From Handmaiden of Colonialism to Esteemed Discipline:

Professor Paul Nchoji Nkwi
on the Reinvention of
Anthropology in Africa

Paul Nchoji Nkwi
in Conversation with
Ivoline Kefen Budji

Langaa Research & Publishing CIG
Mankon, Bamenda

Publisher:
Langaa RPCIG
Langaa Research & Publishing Common Initiative Group
P.O. Box 902 Mankon
Bamenda
North West Region
Cameroon
Langaagrp@gmail.com
www.langaa-rpcig.net

Distributed in and outside N. America by
African Books Collective
orders@africanbookscollective.com
www.africanbookscollective.com

ISBN-10: 9956-551-92-9

ISBN-13: 978-9956-551-92-7

© Ivoline Kefen Budji & Paul Nchoji Nkwi 2021

Table of Contents

Introduction..1
Ivoline Kefen Budji

1. The Journey Towards
   Anthropology...............................17

2. Growth of Anthropology as a
   Discipline in
   Cameroon....................................37

3. The Pan-African Association of
   Anthropologists (PAAA) and
   Collaboration with
   Others..57

4. Anthropology, Tradition, and
   Contemporary Sociopolitical
   Realities.....................................81

5. Applied Anthropology –the Future
   of Anthropology
   in Africa.....................................95

Concluding Remarks......................103
Ivoline Kefen Budji

Afterword....................................105
Paul Nchoji Nkwi

References...107

Paul Nchoji Nkwi: CV &
Publications...113

iv

Introduction

Ivoline Kefen Budji

When I sat down to write an introduction to this work, there was a lot arising from the conversation chronicled within the following pages that I could write about, so much so that it was hard to decide what to focus on and what to leave out. What I knew for certain however was that it would be about the remarkable anthropologist I have been fortunate enough to meet in my lifetime, who has played an indispensable role in the establishment, acceptance, and growth of anthropology as a worthy discipline not just in Cameroon but Africa as a whole: Professor Paul NCHOJI NKWI. Born during the colonial era in Cameroon, Prof, as he is fondly referred to by his peers, colleagues, and students, shares his personal story, which is also the story of colonization (especially within British Cameroons referred to as West or Southern Cameroons), independence, and contemporary nation-building. It is in addition a tale of the establishment of anthropology as well as African anthropologists as respectable, credible, and indispensably useful, in postcolonial Africa.

An anthropology of Africa automatically traces its roots to a colonial and imperialist anthropology and is consequently hardly ever approached from a position of neutrality (Apter 1999). In fact, effects of colonialism are still very much alive and ongoing in contemporary African societies. While it is not my

1

aim to belabour the point already made in many writings about the link between African anthropology and colonialism, permit me to utilize colonialism as a starting point to this introduction and to set the scene for the conversation that follows. Why? Because Prof's early life occurred during this period, which further affected the initial stages of his anthropological career, and because 'the colonial period is more than just an interesting topic for historical research. Ideas that were forged in that context have remained deeply embedded in our analytical frameworks' (Irvine and Gal 2000:72). In addition, while Cameroon was colonized first by the Germans, and then during the First World War, jointly and later separately by the British and the French, thus giving rise to British Cameroons, i.e. present-day anglophone or West/Southern Cameroons, and French Cameroons, i.e. present-day francophone Cameroon (Anchimbe 2018; Ndi 2016), I will focus on British Cameroons chiefly because this was the colonial system under which Prof was born and spent the earlier part of his life, and which contributed to shaping his trajectory and career.

Simply put, earliest anthropologists in sub-Saharan Africa either carried out research within the tenets and protection of colonialism or worked for the colonial government. The presence during this period of anthropologists belonging to colonizer nations doing work in the colonies aggravated the discipline's label as the 'handmaiden of colonialism' (cf. Nkwi and Messina 2015:20; Nkwi 2015a; Barnard 2001; Olukoshi and Nyamnjoh 2011). In fact, the link between the two, i.e. anthropology and colonialism, especially in the British empire, was so great that when colonialism ended, state funding for anthropology and employment of anthropologists in Britain dwindled (Jegede 2015). What these early anthropologists, who mostly belonged to the racialized evolutionary school of thought, wrote about Africa, especially black Africa, apart from informing and often enhancing colonial domination and ideology, also played a major role in propagating the colonially constructed image of Africa (a view still held today by a large part of the world, some anthropologists included), as an inferior and different 'Other' to be 'developed' through the western world's 'civilizing mission in Africa' (Apter 1999: 587; Kallaway 2012; Nyamnjoh 2012).

Anthropologists were needed to provide knowledge of the colonized people's customary laws, structures, and systems so that colonial policies like the British Indirect Rule could be more efficiently implemented (cf. Basu 2016). Even with the emergence of functionalism during the interwar years among anthropologists in British Africa, notions instilled by an evolutionary theoretical perspective were still hard to combat, especially as these ideologies not only changed the structure of African societies, but went further to reconstruct Africa's precolonial history (Apter 1999).

However, and much less mentioned in writings, some anthropologists during this era sometimes shared an ambiguous relationship with the colonial administration. There have been instances of resistance to colonial misappropriation and misuse of information provided as well as blatant refusal to participate in generating information for colonial domination (cf. Apter 1999). A case in point according to Basu (2016) is the controversial Northcote Whitridge Thomas, who was the first anthropologist appointed and sent to work in West Africa between 1909 and 1915 by the British Colonial Office. According to the author, while Northcote supported that anthropology should be indispensable to colonial administration, when asked to research and provide anthropological information about the supposedly cannibalistic Human Leopard Society in Sierra Leone, he declined, as he knew well that the consequence of releasing the cult members' names would be their certain demise.

Following the interconnectedness between anthropology and colonialism, it is no wonder then that after independence, many emerging African nations loathed anthropology and anthropologists (cf. Nkwi and Messina 2015), seeing not just the Western anthropologists who were prominent during the colonial era, but also emerging African anthropologists who had been trained by and in these Western colonizer nations, as untrustworthy and a threat to independent nationhood. It would take a lot of hard work and stamina to change this perception of the discipline within the minds of these new African nation builders. Even at present, many governments and organizations working in different areas of the continent fail to see the essentiality of anthropology in policymaking and nation-building (Ndong, Nde, and Nguo 2015; Nkwi 2015b).

Thus, due to the colonial history of anthropology in Africa, early African anthropologists faced the

4

challenges pathfinders often do, but also some unique to colonized peoples. Having been trained abroad, they had become knowledgeable in anthropological paradigms of the interwar years, e.g., Malinowski's functionalism, Levi-Strauss's structuralism, Radcliffe' Brown's structural functionalism, Boas's historical particularism and cultural relativism, as well as psychocultural theoretical trajectories of Boas's associates like Benedict, Mead, and Sapir, and many other trends (cf. Mcgee and Warms 2017; Nkwi 2015a; Ortner 1984). Many of these budding anthropologists in anglophone colonies (English-speaking or British colonies) were often further divided into either British social anthropologists, American cultural anthropologists, or European ethnologists, depending on the universities and institutions of colonial studies they had been trained in (cf. Barnard 2001; Kallaway 2012; Nkwi and Messina 2015).

Upon their return home in the 1960s and 1970s, a period which coincided with the independence of most African colonies, with the reputation anthropology had gained as a colonial tool, these early African anthropologists had to deal with hostility towards the discipline, as well as the reality of not only different, but often contrasting knowledges, belief systems, outlook, and processes of meaning-making than the ones they had been trained in. Thus, many emigrated or returned to Western universities, and the few who stayed back often identified with the more acceptable and popular social sciences at the time in Africa, thus labelling themselves sociologists, modernists, and/or neo-Marxists (Nkwi 2015a; Nkwi and Messina 2015). This was easy to do because by the 1970s postcolonial theory and Marxism had carved a niche within the discipline of anthropology, as much of the anthropological gaze (especially French and American anthropology) had turned toward real-life problems, prominent among which was the denouncement of the link between anthropology and colonialism/imperialism (Ortner 1984; Ortner 2016).

In British Cameroons the tactic of using anthropological knowledge for colonial rule was more salient especially because of the British colonial policy of Indirect Rule – a policy developed by Lord Lugard, which sought to rule British colonies through their native political structures headed by chiefs or fons (Basu 2016; Ndi 2016; Nkwi 1979). Hence, it was necessary to understand the local people and their political set-up to facilitate the implementation of this policy.

One cannot talk about the anthropology of British Cameroons without mentioning Elizabeth Chilver and Phyllis Kaberry. According to Ardener (1996), Chilver worked as a civil servant in the British Ministry of Economic Warfare and later became Secretary of the Colonial Social Science Research Council concerned with advising research abroad. That is how she met Phyllis Kaberry who at this time (1951) was working as an anthropologist in British Cameroons, and writing the book *Women of the Grassfields*. Ardener elaborates that after accompanying Kaberry to Cameroon in 1958 Chilver eventually undertook several more journeys to the colony, finally producing the book *Traditional*

Bamenda. These two women's works were among the first detailed records of societies in British Cameroons which informed not just the colonial administration, but continue to inform contemporary anthropological studies in Cameroon. In fact, anthropological writings during the colonial period provided a 'database on Africa' (Nkwi 2015b: 622), which is still accessed by many scholars today, whether the aim is to critique or draw from it.

It is within this climate that Prof began his anthropological journey as a trailblazer in both Cameroonian and African anthropology. I remember the first day I met Prof when I had gone to the Catholic University of Cameroon (CATUC) Bamenda for an interview into the Department of Anthropology during the academic year 2011/2012. I was directed to an office where I saw this big man who, unlike many interviewers I had met in my career, sat me down and had a relaxed conversation with me about why I had chosen to pursue a Master's in anthropology, my field of interest, and how anthropology featured in my plans for the future, among others. As time went on my classmates and I (we were the pioneer graduate batch of the department in CATUC) realized just how lucky we were to be having sessions with Prof, who was to us a unique wealth of knowledge. It is no exaggeration to state that if I am today pursuing a PhD in anthropology at the University of Notre Dame, it is thanks to this anthropologist who built a firm foundation for us, who brought anthropology to life for us, and who first introduced me to ethnographic fieldwork and the joys of an inter- and multidisciplinary approach to research.

Commonly referred to as the father of anthropology in Cameroon, Prof would tell us stories about his anthropological journey, which spanned a period of close to 50 years. In his narratives were rich sources of both theory and practice within anthropology. The first ever department of anthropology in Cameroon was started by him in the University of Yaounde, which, according to Nkwi and Messina (2015) was the only university in Cameroon during the 1970s, having come into existence in 1962. The authors further explain that being predominantly fashioned following the French educational system, anthropology was subsumed under sociology and taught often as ethnology, but following the 1993 university reforms, it became recognized as a discipline in its own stead. Over the years the discipline has grown to an accepted field of study in most of the universities in the country, many of which have been started and run either by Prof or his students.

The present work is a conversation I had with Prof about the growth of anthropology in Cameroon and Africa. In our conversation we explore several themes relating to this focus through narratives of Prof's life and journey to anthropology as well as his postdoctoral work in Cameroon and beyond. We also discuss the relevance of anthropology to a 21st century Africa and Cameroon. Here there is a lot of stress on applied anthropology.

Prof takes me through his early beginnings within British Cameroons, how he accesses education during the colonial period, and how this is a life-transforming experience for him. In his narrative, salient issues, apart from the obvious one of Prof's mostly serendipitous journey towards anthropology, include the role of Western religion (specifically Roman Catholicism), not just within colonialism, but also regarding formal education or schooling for the colonized. During the interwar years both Christianity and education were often politicized and deployed to achieve colonial aims (Nkwi 2015; Stambach 2010). Christianity was very prominent within the colonial fabric (cf. Apter 1999; Devisch 2011; Nkwi 1979) often clashing with traditional belief systems (cf. Dureau 2014), and sometimes being incorporated into traditional practices, e.g., burial/funeral rituals (cf. Jindra 2005). This religion was almost always enmeshed with formal education in Africa (Kallaway 2012; Stambach 2010). In fact, 'Western or Christian missionary education has been regarded as one of the most important transformative forces of African societies' (Nkwi 2015: 163).

These two, i.e. Christianity and formal education, played a key role in the British Colonial Office's decision to shift focus on policy advancement in the colonies from being informed by district administrators to being informed by more scientific endeavours, like research geared toward increased African labour and economic produce, and the 'modernization' of the African (Kallaway 2012). Thus, to equip Africans for greater economic productivity and as administrative stooges in the new/modern era being ushered in during this period in the world, the Colonial Office encouraged the education of the colonized, education often carried out in mission schools (Nkwi 2015; Kallaway 2012; Stambach 2010).

In the northwestern Cameroonian Grassfields[1] (found in British Cameroons), where Christianity was introduced in 1903 (Jindra 2005), the colonial administration left all elements of education and character development to missionaries (Ndi 2016). Of special focus within this educational system were young men with a high probability of becoming fons or chiefs (e.g., the sons of chiefs), especially those chiefs who had been appointed as Native Authorities under the Indirect Rule policy (Nkwi 1979). This was in line with Malinowski's recommendations, based on his functionalist approach, of an adaptive education as a means of raising up future Native Authorities within British colonial territories in Africa (Stambach 2010).

This notwithstanding, the colonized peoples of sub-Saharan Africa often actively and agentively incorporated this 'civilizing and modernizing mission' through Christianity and education and utilized it to achieve their own sociopolitical aims. Usually, their main aim was to become empowered in order to interact with, and then challenge, the

---

[1] The Grassfields of Cameroon refers to the predominantly savanna region of the country (today's North West and Western regions) inhabited by over 150 chiefdoms, which though different in terms of languages, lineages, and political structures share certain cultural similarities e.g., regarding gender relations, and connotations and rituals regarding death and mourning – see Funteh and Gormo (2020); Fowler (2011); Jindra (2005).

colonial masters on their home turf (cf. Kallaway 2012). This became glaring during the period of independence, which was often spearheaded by the elite: laypersons who had been educated in the colonial masters' schools and returned to clamour for independence and nationalism (cf. Nkwi 1979). In talking about his experiences, Prof elaborates on these ideas in our discussion, also explaining how African traditional political structure can inform issues of democracy and nationhood in contemporary African countries. To illustrate his point, he uses the *kwifoyn* of the Kom people as an example.

Prof further reflects on the establishment of anthropology as a field of study in the modern state of Cameroon in the late 1970s. Here issues regarding anthropology's sordid past within colonialism as aforementioned, as well as the implications of this perspective on the functioning of the discipline in universities in Africa and other areas of the world which had been previously colonized, e.g., Asia and Latin America, are delved into. A prominent issue also discussed is the difference in educational systems between anglophone and francophone Cameroon, which reflects wider differences in inherited political and sociocultural norms from Cameroon's former colonial masters. Similarly, Prof recounts the creation of another important area of focus: The Pan-African Association of Anthropologists (PAAA). Being instrumental to its formation and growth, Prof describes how the organization came to exist, detailing the role of both African anthropologists and organizations which supported the initiative from the start like the Wenner-Gren Foundation (cf. Nkwi 2015b), and what the PAAA has been able to achieve so far, as well as challenges it faces.

Equally, navigating through theories in anthropology, economics and development, and the social sciences, Prof discusses what the discipline of anthropology means and entails for the Cameroonian and African reality currently fraught with grave political, economic, and sociocultural challenges. It is indeed troubling that the reality of Cameroon today is not much different from that surmised by Ardener (1996) over two decades ago as laden with political, economic, and sociocultural vicissitudes, as well as outside pressures like the current coronavirus pandemic. Cameroon as Africa in miniature showcases the multiculturality and diversity of Africa while illustrating key aspects of interaction with peoples beyond the continent (cf. Ardener 1996), but also shares with Africa and most of the world additional challenges regarding conflict, forced migration and displacement, disease and epidemics, displacement, deforestation, hunger and many others (cf. Devisch 2011; Fonkeng 2019). These are problems of humanity, and therefore problems to which anthropological knowledge can be applied, especially through "'dark anthropology," that is, anthropology that focuses on the harsh dimensions of social life' (Ortner 2016:47). Thus, unlike its history and lesser status in relation to other social science disciplines among African academia (cf. Jegede 2015), anthropology has risen to be respected and indispensable today especially in addressing these issues on the continent.

Regarding the relevance of anthropology both to the present and future Cameroon and Africa, Prof discusses the three perspectives of anthropology: Ivory Tower, Schizoid, and Advocacy. In Africa, there is the tendency to go even beyond Schizoid to Advocacy anthropology as opposed to the Ivory Tower anthropology and its preoccupation with theory, which is more prominent in Western anthropology (Nkwi 2015a). This does not imply that there is no room for theory within African anthropology, only that the more pragmatic Advocacy and applied anthropology are seen as a key and fruitful response to Africa's daily challenges e.g., regarding health and disease (cf. Jegede 2015), as well as a noticeable/visible and practical hallmark to counteract the reputation of anthropology as a colonial tool (Nkwi and Messina 2015; Nkwi 2015a). In fact, anthropology is essential for human development especially rural communities as through its practice, essential background information can be generated for the success of development or planned change initiatives, the lack of which will often lead to catastrophe and failure (Ndong, Nde, and Nguo 2015; Nkwi 2015a).

In this postmodernist era characterized by a critique of knowledge – its production, dissemination, assimilation, and re-production (cf. Mcgee and Warms 2017), the reality of globalization and localization, with multi-vocality and massive information flow (cf. Devisch 2011; Nkwi 2015a), the focus on reflexivity, and the assertion that Western positivism is entangled in systems of culture and control/power (Dureau 2014), where do African anthropologists stand on the world stage? What unique theoretical and practical realities guide their practice? Barnard (2001) in musing over these questions cites Onwuejeogwu's (1975) 'superb blend of British structural-functional theory and African ethnography' (p.168). In the present piece, Prof discusses his idea of an African Pragmatic Socialism as a starting point. He describes this as a form of socialism, which transcends the formulation of theory to a more engaged and practical, advocative, and visible anthropology among African communities – a powerful tool in dispelling the image of anthropology as extractive and imperialistic.

It goes without saying, as Prof points out, that the future of African anthropology lies in its acknowledgment and active projection of the African. The decolonization of this anthropology can be fostered through the 'indigenization and nationalization' (Apter 1999: 591) of the discipline. Africans need to: take the forefront in practicing the anthropology of Africa, listening to and facilitating that the voices of local people be heard i.e. assisting in the production and dissemination of local knowledges; de-westernize the educational process through the introduction of more nuanced and integrative teaching and research designs, which reflect the reality of the African communities they exist in (e.g. languages); provide hands-on/practical and transferable skills trainings/workshops; practice collaboration as well as inter-/multidisciplinary expertise; exercise reflexivity, accommodation, and academic humility; and finally, serve as liaisons, cultural brokers, and/or gatekeepers between Africa and the rest of the world (Barnard 2001; Devisch 2011; Jegede 2015; Nkwi 2015a; Nkwi 2015b; Nyamnjoh 2012). Decolonized knowledge can thus lead to a decolonized university, changing it to a 'pluriversity' i.e., a process of knowledge production that is open to epistemic diversity (Mbembe 2015).

The conversation detailed in this work provides practical examples of some of these proposals. The conversation comprises a series of discussions I had with Prof, the bulk of which took place in August 2017 when he was head of the anthropology department at CATUC. For most of our sessions we would sit adjacent each other with a table between us. His table always had books and papers piled up, and his office shelves were often stacked with more books, papers, and folders. I usually whipped out my audio-recorder and placed it on the table near to Prof, and with my notepad and pen poised to take notes, I would initiate our conversations. Then between 2019 and 2020 we discussed topical issues and events that had occurred after, and which further illuminated, our initial conversations, like his being appointed in 2018 to the Constitutional Council of Cameroon (the body which oversees the constitutionality and application of the laws of the country) and a more detailed discussion of his African Pragmatic Socialism.

The work is divided into five main chapters and a conclusion. I include a sentence or two at the end of each chapter to serve as a signpost about the path the discussion takes as it unfolds. In the conversation recorded here, as with the stories in class, Prof weaves a powerful tale of anthropological thought from an Africanist perspective. This work is therefore relevant for anyone interested in the study and practice of anthropology in Africa.

Chapter 1

The Journey toward Anthropology

Professor Paul NCHOJI NKWI at 70

Ivoline Kefen Budji [henceforth IKB]: *Prof, let us begin by talking about your childhood.*

Paul Nchoji Nkwi [henceforth PNN): Well, I was born in a little village in Komland[2] called Wombong, where I grew up and where I went to school. I must say my father, though not literate or educated, had a great vision and I can see that vision more clearly today than then. I went to school very late according to the standards of today because I first entered the classroom at the age of ten. The simple reason was that the primary school to which my father wanted to send me was about two kilometres away, therefore four kilometres both ways. There were kids much younger than me who covered that distance, but my father thought it was too long for me to trek on a daily basis. Also, being a good and head Christian[3], he had been told that a school would

---

[2] One of four most populous, influential, well-integrated, and prestigious chiefdoms (the other three being Nso, Bali, and Bafut) in the North West Region (which is part of the Cameroonian Grassfields) right from precolonial days, and whose rulers were accorded the status of 'Grade One chiefs' under British colonial rule – see Nkwi (1979)

[3] Christianity in Southern/British Cameroons during this time comprised the Basel, Roman Catholic, and Baptist missions – see Ndi (2016); Nkwi (1979). The Christian religion, precisely Roman Catholicism, which arrived in Kom in 1928, created new hierarchies, as the common man could be 'elevated' in colonial administration and the church if he became a Christian. Choosing Christianity meant gaining access to Western education, ways of dressing, language, and influential positions like catechists, teachers, pupils, interpreters, guides, and

be established a few meters from our compound, which meant that I would simply have to walk a few minutes to get to school. So, I had to wait until I turned ten and a new school was opened in the village, and he personally took me to school[4].

From then things have never been the same because school, i.e. from primary school through secondary school to university, transformed my entire life. I went to secondary school in 1958 at the age of eighteen, and (*with a smile*) nowadays, my grandson is sixteen in Upper Sixth[5]. I went to secondary school as a big boy, an adult of eighteen years old, and I left there in 1963 when I was 23 years old. After secondary school I went on to the Bigard Memorial Seminary in Enugu, Nigeria, where I studied philosophy and theology. However, because of the Biafran war I was sent to the Pontifical Urban

---

retainers commonly called 'mission boys' – see Nkwi (2015). Thus, politics and religion often went together. In fact, the Cameroonian leaders or heads of political parties which rose in the British Cameroons around the time of independence were all practicing Christians – see Ndi (2016).

[4] The first missionary school in Kom, St Anthony's Primary School, was opened by the Mill Hill Missionaries in 1928. By 1939 it was one of only three primary schools found in the whole of British Cameroons, and by the 1950s Kom alone was host to ten missionary schools – see Nkwi (2015).

[5] The final year of high school education in Cameroon. In Upper Sixth students take the qualifying exam called the GCE A/L, i.e. the General Certificate of Education Advanced Level Examination. Upon success they can then move on to higher institutions of learning like universities or professional colleges.

University in Rome from where I graduated with a first degree in theology, with specialization in Christology. That took me all the way to 1971, and from 1971 to 1976 I began my anthropological studies at the Catholic University of Fribourg in Switzerland.

IKB: *Was education back then free of charge or did pupils or students have to pay for it? If it had to be paid for, who paid for your studies at the seminary in Nigeria, your family or some other benefactor?*

PNN: When I look back at those years, I can assert that education was free given the meagre sums that we paid in the primary school system. Under the Indirect Rule policy, which gave local or traditional governance structures power, every adult male paid an education fee plus the poll tax.[6] At the secondary school level, every single student had to pay fees to cover feeding, accommodation and tuition. However, when I went to secondary school at Sasse college[7] in 1958 the fee was about 30 British pounds. That was

---

[6] The British imposed taxation in their African colonies in a bid to raise revenue and improve on the market economy. One of these was the poll tax: a flat rate to be paid by every adult male in the colonial territory. This was enforced through the Native Authorities and their structures – see Gardner (2010); Ndi (2016).

[7] St Joseph's College, Sasse, Buea, popularly referred to as 'Sasse' or 'Sasse College', was one of the early colleges opened by the Roman Catholics in Southern Cameroons – see Ndi (2016).

a lot of money and my parents were able to pay my school fee only for the first year. So, at the end of that year, my father approached the Kom Area Cooperative Union (KACU), a farmers' organization to which he and my mother belonged, and asked about the possibility of awarding a scholarship for his son. The organization granted his request. Much later, upon completion of my studies at Sasse, when I went on to study for the priesthood in Enugu, Nigeria, the Diocese of Buea bore all the expenses, assisted by a Canadian benefactor, Mr Lawrenz Bens, who virtually adopted me as his son. In fact, upon his death in 1978 it was revealed that he had willed part of his estate to me, most of which I used in 1989 to establish the *Georgian City Academy* (GCA), a technical school for young men and women in Boyo Division where Komland is situated. This explains why GCA became the lowest paying school system in the entire Boyo Division within the North West Region of Cameroon.

IKB: *Ok, so did you study theology and philosophy at Enugu because you wanted to become a priest back then?*

PNN: Definitely. I did three solid years of philosophy and five years of theology. Only God knows why He brings you up to a point and then changes your path. I should have been a priest in 1971 because I underwent all the training and did all the preparations, but on the eve of my becoming a deacon, after talking with my spiritual director, Fr. Salgado, he said, 'Paul I want you to take a year off, go somewhere new, and study something else.' And this spiritual director single-handedly found a scholarship for me and sent me to the University of Fribourg, where I discovered anthropology and where I stayed for six years studying in the discipline.

Students of Georgian City Academy (founded by Prof Nkwi in 1989) and some title holders at the celebration of Prof's final initiation into the kwifoyn, the male regulatory society in Komland (Kom – Cameroon, 1992)

IKB: *When you say you discovered anthropology...?*

PNN: Yea, actually, the training in the seminary is generally such that the church insists that seminarians or people studying for the priesthood should study anthropology, because their work of evangelization must be built on a better knowledge of the culture of the people they will serve as priests. So, knowing the people and knowing their culture prepares a priest better for his work in God's vineyard. Therefore, anthropology is effectively taught in the seminary. In

22

fact, when I began to study theology, we had this priest, Professor Akoi from Ghana, who was responsible for teaching anthropology to seminarians preparing for the priesthood. Another of the priests who taught us was Professor Grotannelli, who was Professor at the University of Rome. I became fascinated with the courses they taught us regarding anthropology as the study of culture. Even though these courses were not elaborate or extensive enough, Professors Grotannelli and Akoi taught them in an attempt to introduce the discipline and make us understand what culture was all about.

During my philosophical and theological training, both priests began to push me toward a better understanding of what anthropology entailed and what human culture was all about. Grotannelli defined culture as, 'The conscious and deliberate activity of man as a human being and as a rational being, and all the concrete and abstract manifestations that belong to us or belong to a group as a group.' I was fascinated by this definition and have continued to use it to illustrate the diversity and richness of culture.

And so, when I finished school, I got my STM, which is the licentiate or honours degree acquired after a four-year period of studying sacred theology.

One thing I need to emphasize here is that while doing those introductory courses in anthropology I began to read anything I could find that had been written about my own people, specifically about Kom. I realized that there were two anthropologists who had written quite a bit about the Kom people: Elizabeth Chilver, we sometimes call her Sally

Chilver, who taught at Lady Margaret Hall, Oxford, and another anthropologist, what is the name...

IKB: *Do you mean Phyllis Kaberry?*

PNN: Yes! Phyllis Kaberry. Those two. Phyllis Kaberry did most of her work among the Nso people, but the two of them collectively did a lot of ethnography on the Grassfields. You know the famous book on *Traditional Bamenda* was written by Chilver, who also wrote several articles on Kom. In fact, a famous article co-written by these two women was published in the book *West African Kingdoms of the nineteenth Century*, a book edited by Daryll Forde and Phyllis Kaberry.[8]

So, I began to read what these two ladies were writing. First, I was not just fascinated by what I was reading but I was also intrigued by the fact that they as foreigners were interested in the culture of the Kom people, and that they were making an attempt to capture that culture in written form. And then I began to ask myself, 'Why should I not do the kind of work that they are doing?'

Therefore, I came to anthropology through the inspiration of these two women – Phyllis Kaberry and Sally Chilver, although Grotannelli and Akoi had led me to discover Kaberry and Chilver. And so, I decided to study anthropology on the scope that I would write a better description of our culture than

---

[8] This book was first published in 1967 by the International African Institute, and more recently in 2018 by Routledge. Chilver and Kaberry's article in the book is titled: *'The Kingdom of Kom in West Cameroon.'*

these people who did not know the Kom language, and who were attempting to understand my people. So, I thought, 'Let me go in there and do the work that they should have done, and I will do it much better because I speak Kom and I can easily control, verify, and synthesize information given to me by my own people.' That is how I came to anthropology. It was a challenge to me by these two great ladies. Once, I wrote to them and said, 'I want to do anthropology,' and they responded, 'Please come to University of London and do anthropology here under us.' I travelled to London, I met them through the department, but then they did not have the money to sponsor me, and I could not get a scholarship to study there. We are talking around 1970 – 1971.

So, back to my journey to Switzerland. As I said before, once I got the STM, my spiritual director, Fr. Salgado said, 'Look, go and do a secular subject. Go to Switzerland. Here is a scholarship for you. Everything is taken care of.' Everything, I mean virtually everything! They paid me to go to school, cleaned my room and clothes, fed me, and gave me pocket allowance. I didn't have to do anything other than study. So, there was no reason to fail. It was the best scholarship. And the rule of the scholarship then was that if you didn't pass your exam you were parcelled and sent back to your country. And therefore, instead of going to University College in London and studying under Phyllis Kaberry, or going to Oxford, and studying under Chilver, I got this scholarship to go to Switzerland. So, I went to the University of Fribourg and found the department of ethnology.

There, I met Professor Hugo Huber who was then the head of the department of ethnology at the University of Fribourg, and he was a priest too! So, I was very lucky. I had moved from the seminary into the hands of a priest. My training had previously been supervised by priests and here I had landed to study anthropology under a priest. In fact, the department was run by two priests and a teaching assistant. Who were these two priests and why were they anthropologists? They were the disciples of the founder of the *kulturhistorische methode* translated as the cultural historical method, which is the main diffusionist theory[9] in anthropology, founded by the Divine Word Fathers and shaped, again, by priests, Pater Wilhelm Schmidt and Fr. Koppers. The Divine Word Fathers were missionaries, and from their travels and work in various areas of the world, had sought to explain culture as having diffused from a given centre to new centres. The diffusionist trend in anthropology was designed to counter the evolutionist theory, because the evolutionist theory of Tylor and Morgan said that societies or social institutions had evolved from simple to more complex structures and that explained similarities between cultures.

Now let us restate what the whole issue was. Within the Age of Discovery when Europeans went out to explore the rest of the world and came back with stories about parallels among cultures,

---

[9] For more about theory in anthropology especially more contemporary theorizing, and the evolution of anthropology as a discipline, see Mcgee and Warms (2017).

somebody had to explain, why on earth, there were cultural similarities in places that were far apart. Why would you find pyramids in Egypt and among the Incas in South America? How come? Tylor and Morgan would say, well, it was because of evolution: social institutions had evolved through time and state. But the people I studied under were diffusionists and they said, 'Look here, it is not evolution. It is because cultural elements migrate from one place to another, and therefore the similarities you are finding are not because of evolution but migration. The idea of building a pyramid could have migrated from the Egyptians all the way to South America. So, according to the cultural historical method, you can take all social institutions and systematically study them carefully. You will identify that cultural elements that are similar migrated from one point to another. You can look at the quality, form, and content of the elements you are studying, and if they are similar, then there is the possibility that cultural migration has taken place.'

Do not forget that these were priests, and they were working against the backdrop of the Bible, which records that at one point, Eve and Adam were thrown out of the Garden. In fact, initially the *kulturhistorische methode* believed and circulated the thinking that all cultures probably developed in the Garden of Eden. And when the first people were thrown out of the Garden they began to spread throughout the world and bring these different cultures to different places. That was the initial attempt to explain cultural diffusion. However, proponents later began to back out of that theory of paradise, but they didn't think of using other rational ways of reflecting. They maintained their diffusionist theory but did not hold that cultures all came from the Garden of Eden.

So, I studied under this school of anthropology called the cultural historical method, which was the German-Austrian school of thought within anthropology. However, I would break ranks with them once I got my PhD. This was because while I was studying ethnology at the university under these disciples of Fr. Wilhelm Schmidt, I read more of what was coming out from the anthropology of the Americas. So, in a sense I broke ranks with the methods I had been taught as I studied under European anthropology and began to look at the form of anthropology that was being taught and practiced elsewhere especially in the US.

IKB: *What was it about American anthropology that so fascinated you that you would prefer it to, say British or European anthropology, under which, as you say, you had been trained for years?*

PNN: In Britain they talked more about social anthropology, which in a nutshell was a focus on the social institutions that governed any human culture. In America they used a much broader word – cultural anthropology. I found that more encompassing. So, I found myself tilting more towards cultural anthropology and its growth to incorporate four sub-specializations. The Americans had a much broader vision, which I admired and subscribed to. You had biological or physical anthropology, you had cultural anthropology, and then you had archaeology, and linguistics. I found that much more fascinating. On the other hand, while the British practiced social anthropology, on continental Europe what was known as anthropology was physical anthropology. When you mentioned anthropology, people in France, for example, would immediately think you were referring to physical anthropology. Cultural anthropology or social anthropology was just considered as part of sociology. This view of anthropology was so dominant in France that the few Africans who had set out to study especially cultural anthropology in that country returned home as sociologists rather than anthropologists. So, I was more attracted to the way anthropology was being practiced in the USA, and that is the trend that has inspired me throughout. In fact, after my PhD, in my teaching career and in my practice, I have worked more with the Americans than I have with the people who trained me.

IKB: *What was your PhD research about?*

PNN: I did a thesis on political anthropology. The reason I focused on political anthropology was again my fascination with the involvement of traditional chiefs in modern politics and the conscious engagement of the British in getting chiefs involved in defining the future of modern British Cameroons. I began to look at the Lord Lugard policy,[10] which

---

[10] Lord Lugard served as the British Governor of the Southern Nigeria Protectorate (1912 – 1914) under which Southern Cameroons was later administered. He coined and

advised the colonial government not to disrupt traditional structures of governance but to use them in running the colonies. Therefore, the famous policy of Indirect Rule simply said, 'We can find comparable political institutions in Africa to help us govern our colonies instead of installing new structures.' And so, the whole idea of Native Authorities[11] or the NA, was to empower these structures to work closely with colonial officers in governing the colonies.

During the 1950s and 1960s, as the British were withdrawing and preparing to hand over the territory to new nationalist leaders, i.e., Endeley, Jua, Foncha etc.,[12] the problem was what would become of those Native Authorities that the colonial government had used to colonize the colonies. Would the chiefs be

---

propagated the idea of a 'dual mandate' among British colonies in Africa, which essentially meant merging colonial and African traditional administrative elements. The resulting policy was Indirect Rule – see Basu (2016); Kallaway (2012); Nkwi (1979).

[11] Already existing African chiefs and their political structures, who were appointed by the British to oversee the administration of their people and other peoples placed under them on behalf of the British; in essence they ruled these people but were answerable to the British – see Nkwi (1979); Stambach (2010).

[12] See Ndi (2016) and Doho (2020) for more information about these individuals, their political parties, and their role in the rise of nationalism and the resulting independence from British colonial rule in Southern Cameroons, e.g. Endeley – KNC, Foncha – KNDP, Muna – CUC, Kale and Mbile – KPP, and Jua – Prime Minister of the State of West Cameroon from 1965 – 68.

part of the new government or would they be pushed aside? Therefore, in the conferences that were held prior to the independence of British Cameroons in London, in Nigeria, and in Cameroon we had chiefs, also called Fons. Galega, Fon of Bali, and other fons in the North West were part of the negotiations, and we would eventually see the new form of government which would have the House of Assembly and the House of Chiefs. In this way all those guys who had worked and assisted the British as Native Authorities would be given room to participate in running this emerging country. Thus, they created the House of Chiefs where chiefs could be represented, and the House of Assembly for elected leaders. So, this was the climate we had in the 1950s and 1960s.

Hence, in the 1970s when I started preparing to do my PhD in anthropology, I thought it would be exciting to focus just on one chiefdom, the Kom people, and to examine Kom political institutions – what they were, how they functioned, and how they could be part of an emerging modern system[13]. My thesis was entitled: *Traditional Government and Social Change*, because the Kom kingdom or the fon or king of Kom was part of the Native Authority structure that had been set up by the British government. The British used those Native Authorities to collect taxes, build roads, and provide social services. So, my focus was to examine the Kom kingdom, study it, look at what Chilver and Kaberry had done with respect to politics, and then see how the traditional leaders and

---

[13] For more information about the Kom fondom and palace, see Nkwi (1985).

the modern elite were trying to participate in shaping the emergence of modern Southern Cameroons.

I also looked at the role of people like Augustine Ngom Jua, a son of Kom who later became Prime Minister.[14] Jua got into the House of Assembly and became involved in modern politics after having served on the Native Authority Council for the Wum division. He had been chosen by the Fon of Kom to represent him at the Council, and it was from there that he gained more and more power to get into politics. So, my thesis looked at this transformation, i.e., what the real political structures of Kom were, how they were used by the British, traditional rulers, and modern politicians, and how they would emerge and become part and parcel of an emerging nation.

Towards finishing up my PhD thesis I was employed as a teaching assistant at the Catholic University of Fribourg. That was really my first professional appointment by the state of Fribourg. I stayed there just for about six months and left because I wanted to come back to Cameroon. However, if I had not married, I would probably never have returned to Cameroon. So, I dropped that job and came back to Cameroon, where I spent the next six months trying to get a job as a researcher in the Institute of Human Sciences in Yaounde[15]. It did not work out and I finally got into teaching.

---

[14] See note 12 above

[15] Political capital of the modern state of Cameroon situated in the Centre Region of the country, predominantly French speaking.

So, when you ask who I am, I am simply a small village boy whose life was completely transformed by the kind of education my parents and my benefactors gave me. I am the product of the kindness and the love of lots of people who probably didn't know what I would be, but who believed in a system that could transform individuals… individuals who can serve their society, and I think I am today just an instrument of societal transformation.

IKB: *I am intrigued by the role of Christianity, in terms of education and benefactors, in your training and anthropological career. I have sometimes had conversations with some young people who say that the more they study anthropology, the more they question the existence of God and the whole idea of religion, choosing to see these, as many scholars have debated about before, as an invention to explain the currently unexplainable[16]. Therefore, what is your take on the assertion that the more scientific a person's mind becomes the less place religion has in that person's life?*

PNN: I don't subscribe to that thinking because having studied theology in-depth and specialized even in an area called Christology, my vision of religion is not just an attempt by each human group to explain some of the unexplainable phenomena, but that religion gives us an opportunity to discover who we are, where we came from, and where we are going

---

[16] For more about the debates regarding religion and science/reason, see Asad (1993).

to. These questions are some of the fundamental questions that each human group, or each human culture must address. So, religion is not limited only to Catholicism, or Christianity, or Islam, but refers to a whole system of beliefs that tends to explain those three fundamental questions. Having been brought up as a Christian and a Catholic, my greater understanding, and my exploration of the intellectual and academic world, have effectively enriched my religious commitment, rather than made me more … how would you call it… lax, or changed the notion of God I was brought up in and that I still believe. I would say that this reflection on religion has led me to conclude that science is an attempt to discover the truth, and that truth is God. So, if we do not discover that truth and make it part of our life, religion becomes meaningless. I think it was Neil Armstrong who, when he landed on the moon and returned – I hope I am quoting him rightly – simply said God exists. I mean, we humans have explored the world beyond, we have devised ways and been to the moon, but our little brains can never fully understand the depth of what and who God is. Therefore, I think that science slowly and gradually helps us understand God.

The day we will fully discover the truth of what God is, I believe the world will end, because there will be nothing more to discover. The more we learn about sciences, about this world, what we are, the more we begin to understand the complexity of God's creation. Issues about cloning of people and animals, issues regarding stem cell research, all these issues about trying to understand the structure of the human cell and how it functions, all of these are ways to seek the truth. Even if we succeed to recreate the natural, all our scientific endeavour is geared toward understanding truth. Hence, I believe that creating and disseminating knowledge should rather enrich our understanding and appreciation of what religion is. As Christians we believe that Christ came to tell us a little more about himself and God, to confirm some of the things that we always believed. Christ's coming widened our narrow view of life, religion, and God.

This belief in the supernatural is not restricted to Western religion. In the traditional belief of the Kom people, for example, heaven and hell exist. These concepts were not introduced when Christianity came. The precolonial Kom people knew that the good and the bad existed. According to our theodicy, evil exists, good exists, and the two cannot co-exist. My culture explains that when those who are bad people die, they go to a place where there is no life, where nothing grows. So, they go to the so-called red soil. Conversely, when they die, the good people go to a place where life is in abundance, where you can grow anything, where you have a better life.

This concept of religion has fascinated me, us in anthropology, and all human groups. Hence, anthropologists have over the years gone back to the study ancient religions. These studies demonstrate to us that religion is a key component of our lives, and therefore we should not discard it from our own way of life.

IKB: *These views on Christianity conclude the introductory chapter. In the next chapter, our conversation focuses on Prof's* *return to Cameroon as an anthropologist, exploring the development of anthropology as a discipline not just in the University of Yaounde I, but in the rest of Cameroon.*

Chapter 2

Growth of Anthropology as a Discipline in Cameroon

IKB: *So, upon the completion of your studies, and having worked for six months in Fribourg you returned to Cameroon and started teaching at the University of Yaounde I.*

PNN: It was then University of Yaounde[17]. There was only one university in Cameroon at the time.

IKB: *Ok, thanks for straightening that out. You said upon your arrival from Fribourg you spent six months trying to get a job that was focused on research. Does that mean that your interest was not to lecture at the university?*

PNN: Not initially. At first, when I just returned, I did not want to go into teaching, I wanted to do research. I wanted to go out there, you know, and do research in an institution, and publish, and so I applied to the Institute of Human Sciences, but they never gave me the job. Therefore, I walked over to

---

[17] The university acquired the name University of Yaounde I in 1993 when, because of university reforms in the country, other universities were opened, and so the University of Yaounde became split into the University of Yaounde I (the mother university which stayed at Ngoa Ekele), and the University of Yaounde II in Soa, both in Yaounde – see Nkwi and Messina (2015).

the University of Yaounde and the guys said, 'We have been looking for somebody to teach, or to take care of anglophones in the department of Sociology.' That is how I got in. Professor Jean Mfoulou single-handedly dragged me into the department of Sociology. So, I was recruited, and I started teaching basic courses in anthropology on 01 October 1976.

IKB: *Predominantly to anglophones?*

PNN: No, no. Actually, I was brought in there first to give a chance to English speakers at the university to have somebody in the department whom they could liaise with, and secondly to take up all related subjects of an anthropological nature, like Introduction to Anthropology. And at that time what they wanted me to do which I always found uhm... strange, is that they wanted me to teach the sociology of traditional Africa. What was the reality at the time I joined teaching at the University of Yaounde, this is in 1976, was that Yaounde University was barely fourteen years old, and the course that was introduced in the faculty of Arts was Sociology. They taught Sociology and they taught Philosophy. Anthropology as a discipline did not exist. They may have introduced a few courses in marriage and kinship, but anthropology as anthropology was not part of the university curriculum.

The university did not want to use the word anthropology because, well, that word anthropology was seen as a dirty word in the sense that anthropology had been used as an instrument of colonization. It was a handmaiden of colonialism. And when placed in that context you begin to see why

Sally and Kaberry did the kind of work that they did in the North West. It was in the North West Region that the two of them generated monographs like *Traditional Bamenda*, to inform the British colonial administration as to what the social structures of these regions were. Jeffries himself who was one of the colonial administrators also got interested in anthropology, and he became an anthropologist. Since this was the case in many areas of the African continent, anthropology acquired a bad name not only in Cameroon but throughout Africa. It was a dirty word, especially beginning from the 1960s through the 1970s, because the nationalist leaders, people who were fighting for the independence of Africa, saw anthropology as a discipline of subjugation, a discipline that went out to make the colonialists understand what local people were about, so that they would better rule them.

But again, one thing I need to note is that African countries began to gain independence in the 1960s. During this period, the nationalist leaders wanted to rid Africa of the colonial yoke. Anything related to colonialism had to be dealt with to such an extent that some of us who were already studying anthropology in the 1960s and in the 1970s would prefer to call ourselves Marxist anthropologists, because Marxism was never associated with colonialism. It was perceived in a more favourable light as an orientation that could be utilized to fight colonialism. So, most of us went around, at least my generation in the 1970s, calling ourselves Marxist anthropologists even though we were not Marxists. The more marketable title to use was to refer to yourself as a Marxist anthropologist. Most, and I still believe that this applies to quite a lot of my colleagues at the time who were teachers in the university, who claimed they were Marxists today are not. But it was a better word to use, Marxist, as opposed to the word anthropologist.

In 1973 I was still preparing to do fieldwork among the Kom people. And in that year the first conference of African scientists met in Algiers, Algeria, and banned anthropology from university curricula, in 1973! This meant that any African university that had anthropology or anything related to colonialism was strongly advised to have it removed from the school's curriculum. So, you would then understand. Here I am coming into the University of Yaounde and I am told to teach the sociology of traditional Africa, which was like saying instead of calling it anthropology or cultural anthropology, they would call it the sociology of traditional Africa. I said, 'Ok, fine.' And I used to joke with my students, having been adopted into the Marxist tradition, I always told them I was not a Marxist but that I truly believed in African Pragmatic Socialism. That is what I call my own brand of socialism[18]. So, don't call me Marxist. Instead, call me an African pragmatic socialist, which simply means we can help the communities in which we reside to live a better life without exploiting the weak and the poor, but making sure that all share in an equitable manner the resources and all the benefits that accrue

---

[18] For a more in-depth understanding of theory within African anthropology, see Mafeje (1976).

from our collective work. Note here that my emphasis is on the community, not the individual.

When I started working at the university, the students in the whole department were not up to 30 in number. Because it was a small group, it was easy for me to gather them and begin introducing the discipline of anthropology, specifically cultural anthropology. In addition, I would take them out of the classroom for fieldwork. I remember I would take them as far as the Eastern province[19], and drop them off in villages, come back every two days to visit them, talk to them, and train them on how to collect, transcribe, and analyse data. And the students were very happy... very happy. But then some of my colleagues, sociologists, would actively tell students that anthropologists studied primitive people, that anthropology did not have a position in modern Cameroon, and that it had no role to play in the development of a modern nation. Maybe that was what kept our numbers minimal. However, the students who continued in anthropology are today doing great work for the nation and beyond.

IKB: *Were these colleagues, sociologists?*
PNN: Yes, sociologists. Their comments did not however deter me.

---

[19] The old word for Region in Cameroon. Cameroon has ten regions – eight which were colonized by the French and are predominantly French-speaking, and two, i.e., the North West and South West, which were colonized by the British and are predominantly English-speaking.

Also, although my basic training was in cultural anthropology, and political anthropology is just a small part of it, as I began to engage myself in teaching, my interest in other areas began to develop. Don't forget that I was hired in 1976 and by 1980 I was appointed as a government official. I became Program Officer in the Ministry of Scientific and Technical Research in Cameroon, and I served in that capacity and several others within the ministry for eight years. During this time, I was Program Officer, Deputy Director, Acting Director, and Senior Adviser. These positions forced me to open myself to other critical areas of an applied nature in anthropology. And what were these critical areas? Mostly medical anthropology and development anthropology. I think these were the two critical areas that widened my practice of anthropology.

Furthermore, my leaning towards applied anthropology was enhanced when I participated in the World Conference on Cultural Policies which took place in Mexico in 1982 while I was working as an official in the ministry. In this conference were people from all over the world who had converged in Mexico to ask big questions, for example, finding out why development and social transformation had failed in Africa. Why was it that so much money was being poured into Africa, but no significant change was being seen? Had the modernization theory failed, or why had the modernization theory failed, to achieve the same result it had achieved elsewhere?

Prof Nkwi (front left, holding a file folder) as Deputy Director for Scientific Research, with senior officials of the Ministry of Scientific and Technical Research (Douala – Cameroon, 1988)

The modernization theory crafted by economics and sociology simply said science was the best way to achieve social transformation and that was how other countries had developed in Europe and the rest of the world. But projects built on this theory and implemented in Africa and many other colonies had not achieved the same level of development despite the massive investments in them. Because it was stated in the modernization theory that industrialization was key, any country that could industrialize itself would develop. So, the logic had been to create industries in Africa. However, most of them had ended in failure. Of course, if I had been consulted as an anthropologist, I would have pointed out that this was mostly because the cultural beliefs and practices of the residents where these projects were carried out had not been taken into consideration when the projects were being implemented. For example, when you create an industry among the pygmies and you expect to use their labour, it won't work simply because they will not give you the labour you are counting on.

What I am driving at here is that the conference in 1982, they called it *Mondiacult*, indexed culture as a key factor of development, but which had been neglected in the development process of Africa. It was at this juncture that culture took centre stage, and by bringing culture unto the centre stage, the conference indirectly indexed the discipline concerned with the teaching and understanding of culture, i.e., anthropology. You'll see that after that conference in Mexico, most international organizations, the UN organizations, WHO, UNESCO, UNFPA, and other international NGOs started turning to culture to resolve some of the basic problems of Africa's development, whether these problems were environmental, health-related, or affecting other areas of development, growth, and wellbeing. Sometimes I look at the Mexico conference as one of the flashpoints of anthropology, because after that there was increased interest in anthropology and what anthropology could do. If we go back to 1971 there were three anthropologists at the World Bank, three anthropologists! But go from that period to 1982 and later and the number begins to increase.

Therefore, in the 1980s, consulting possibilities for anthropologists increased almost exponentially, but there were very few anthropologists available. And who were these anthropologists? They were not African. The guys who were running around Africa trying to do good work in anthropology and doing consultancy were from Europe and America. This was the point where some of us began to believe in a future for African anthropology, and to actively reshape our programs and curricula. At least speaking for myself, I began to reorient my program to teach appropriate subjects that would help my students compete and work in competitive fields. That is why we introduced courses like project design and implementation, environmental anthropology, medical anthropology, and development anthropology, and these again helped to expand the numbers of students who joined our department.

By the time I retired in 2006 from the University of Yaounde, now the University of Yaounde I, we had over 900 students taking anthropology at all levels, as compared to the 30 when I started teaching anthropology. Also, at this time, anthropology was being taught as a discipline separate from sociology. By 1993 – 94 the discipline could award degrees, i.e., first degrees in anthropology, because the university reforms of 1993 – 94 offered anthropology this possibility. So, by 2006 it had emerged as a full department.

Today, the attitude of the 1960s to regard anthropology as studying native peoples has changed, nobody even talks about that because we have now turned the discipline from a discipline that studied the 'Other' to a discipline that studies the 'Self'[20]. Earlier

---

[20] For more about anthropological views regarding 'Self', 'Other', 'Being', and the ontological turn, see Vigh and Sausdal (2012).

anthropologists had come out to study other cultures. That era had passed and now we were training a new crop of anthropologists who would be studying their own societies, and I was a typical example when I began to study and do anthropological work among my own people.

IKB: *So, after having helped to set up the anthropology department in Yaounde, upon your retirement, you came to Bamenda[21] where you took an active role in setting up the anthropology department at the Catholic University of Cameroon, Bamenda. If you look at the two of them: Yaounde and Bamenda, would you say that you faced different challenges depending on whether it was in the francophone section or the anglophone section? I ask this because the sociopolitical and cultural norms handed down by colonialism, for example the French indigenat, prestation, and civil law, and the British indirect rule and common law are different. Would you say that this difference in colonial legacies has affected the way the institutions have been set up, and the running of the anthropology program in different areas of the country?*

PNN: Definitely. To begin with, in my early years at University of Yaounde, I could feel the resistance and the critique of our francophone brothers who

---

[21] The capital of the North West Region of Cameroon, which together with the South West Region are the only two Anglophone Regions colonized by the British.

thought anthropology was physical anthropology. Any other thing was sociology. But I went on to insist that cultural anthropology existed and that was what I taught as I tried to make an impact. One interesting thing during my stay there, which I must mention, was that in 1978 they wanted to scrap sociology and anthropology from the university curriculum. We were called to a meeting in the vice chancellor's office and told to revise our program and obliterate anthropology. And what I did – I was acting Head of Department then – was that I called a meeting of the department and we wrote an eight-page protest justifying why sociology and anthropology needed to stay on the school curriculum. We crafted the letter in such a way that we quoted paragraphs from congresses of Union Camerounaise (UC) which was Ahidjo's party[22], where he had emphasized the teaching of sociology and psychology. We asked within the letter, 'Has government changed its mind from studying some of these fundamental subjects? We ask because this morning during a meeting at the university we were instructed to remove some of them from our program.' We took a copy straight to the presidency and dropped another copy at the Ministry of Higher Education. The following day the chancellor of the university received a call from the presidency which said, 'Please don't start another strike. Put back their subject on the curriculum.'

---

[22] For more about the UC, Ahidjo, and the crafting of the modern Cameroonian nation after independence, see Ndi (2016).

IKB: *Did the strike the presidency was referring to have anything to do with the Structural Adjustment Program and reforms in the educational system in the late 1970s and 1980s, which called for a merging of anthropology and sociology into one degree under the banner of philosophy, or was there something else going on?*

PNN: In the 1980s due to increasing unemployment of university graduates, the concept of professionalization was imposed on the lone University of Yaounde. Disciplines that lacked employability capacity such as sociology and anthropology became victims of academic reforms. How could these disciplines train students to find immediate employment upon graduation? The Structural Adjustment Programs (SAP) of Bretton Wood Institutions were designed to build in costs-saving measures into governments programs: increase in tuition, elimination of disciplines that lacked employability potential, and the imposition of cost recovery measures. All these can be summarized as getting people to pay for services once offered free of charge. The strike I referred to here, reminds us of the strike by most Anglophone students over attempts by the Ministry of Education to abolish the GCE examination system. It was not advisable for university authorities to carry out reforms that would lead to unrest again.

I must say that my stay in Yaounde for those 30 years wasn't very easy. However, fourteen of those years were spent in the government ministry, and that was good for me because I was right in the middle of policymaking machinery, and I could shape and orient or define policy. Working in that policymaking position probably helped me keep the discipline alive. And people respected my views on the necessity of integrating social sciences in whatever we did. Nevertheless, even here, some of my francophone co-workers constantly told me that we were training people whose job marketability was nil. I kept telling them about the work anthropologists could do if they were trained more in the applied areas. But those years... they were very difficult.

Then I retired and came to CATUC. I was lucky to have retired in 2006 and by 2007 already be working on a new project, the creation of CATUC. I was indeed given the opportunity to partake in the new university's conceptualization. I just told myself that if I wasn't satisfied with the way anthropology was being taught and used in Cameroon, this was the finest opportunity to do something better and different. So, I decided to create a department of anthropology. This was easy because while teaching at the University of Yaounde I, I had also taught anthropology at the Catholic University of Central Africa in Yaounde, and at the St. Thomas Aquinas Seminary in Bambui, Bamenda. In addition, being in a Catholic environment gave me the opportunity to shape programs in ways that I couldn't do elsewhere. By chairing the committee or the think tank that created CATUC in Bamenda, I had a free hand. I was very proud of this new initiative.

Matriculation at the Catholic University of Cameroon (CATUC) Bamenda, where Prof Nkwi was Deputy Vice Chancellor, and Head of the Anthropology Department (Bamenda – Cameroon, 2010)

Taking our conversation back to Yaounde, I need to remark that the department of anthropology at the University of Yaounde I has given birth to at least four departments. There's a department of anthropology at the University of Buea[23], a department of sociology and anthropology at the University of Douala[24], and then the department of anthropology at CATUC. That means you have Yaounde, Buea, Douala, and Bamenda. At one point the University of Bamenda asked me to design a program for anthropology, and I did. Probably it is in the making but some day somehow, anthropology will be part of the institution. So, the discipline of anthropology has grown, and continues to grow in Cameroon. It needs to make its mark by doing good ethnographic work, or in short fulfilling the three basic functions of a university, which are teaching, research, and outreach. If we can design good programs, do really good teaching, do good research, and then do outreach by being more committed in the communities we work with, we will be serving our communities and people, while helping to move not just the discipline, but the whole nation forward.

IKB: *Indeed. So, apart from anthropology being finally accepted as a credible discipline as opposed to the 1960s and 1970s, and the discipline starting in Yaounde and then spreading to other Cameroonian universities, have there been other significant changes that have occurred in the study and practice of*

---

[23] The capital of the South West Region of Cameroon, which together with the North West Region are the only two Anglophone Regions colonized by the British.

[24] The economic capital of Cameroon situated in the Littoral Region of the country.

anthropology in Cameroon from the 1960s till now?

PNN: One of the most significant changes has been a better understanding of what anthropology is and what anthropology can do. When I began teaching at the University of Yaounde and working within the academic world at a time that was hostile to anthropology, my strong belief was that anthropology could only redeem itself from the colonial image if it played a critical role in the transformation of the lives of people among whom we worked. Therefore, my emphasis was that applied anthropology would become the saviour of the discipline. Applied anthropology would be used as a tool to clean anthropology from its dirty image, would take off this mark of the maiden of colonialism. My emphasis here is that we can show the relevance of anthropology through applied areas. So, for example, anthropological knowledge can contribute greatly towards addressing issues regarding HIV/ AIDS, among others. I began to introduce those applied areas in Yaounde, and I think that this was a significant contribution. The significant change here is that in all the departments that have been created in state universities and in private universities in Cameroon, the emphasis has been on applied anthropology.

One thing I have always said is that we anthropologists or anybody in the social sciences, write our theses and dissertations about a people, we get our PhDs, and we go on to get good jobs, but we never think about the people who educated us, because the material that you used to shape and write your own thesis and to craft your own theories, was provided by people. We as anthropologists should never forget that the people who taught us and brought us to this level are those key informants. We should never forget that. And this is where my African Pragmatic Socialism comes in, that there can never be a total withdrawal from the communities in which we work, the communities that provided us with the knowledge, the communities that made us what we are. We need always to think about that, and be more pragmatic, because those communities have health problems, social problems, economic problems. If we can use the knowledge we collected and analysed and got our PhDs to help them, to uplift their standards, we will be making a big contribution. I think this is the major shift in anthropology, which I have encouraged throughout my life, or throughout my at least 40 years of teaching and practicing anthropology.

IKB: *And now that you are a member of the Constitutional Council of Cameroon, have you retired from teaching, and if you have, how do you feel about that?*

PNN: It was in February 2018 that I was appointed by the Head of State as a member of the Constitutional Council, the body that rules on the constitutionality of laws in Cameroon as well as treaties and international agreements. To be honest with you, it came to me as a surprise and took me away from a job I like most, a job I had been doing for 42 years, that is since I was hired in October 1976 to teach anthropology at the lone University of

Yaounde. When I retired in 2006, I thought I was done with teaching. Little did I know I would spend the next twelve years engaged in teaching and administration at the newly created CATUC, Bamenda.

My appointment as a member of the Constitutional Council took me out of the classroom but I did not abandon my PhD students, whom I continued to supervise. Of the five PhD students I was working with at the time of my appointment, two defended their theses in 2019, and one is currently under review and should defend by July 2020. I really enjoyed teaching because it did not only permit me to keep abreast with the growing knowledge in anthropology, but it allowed me to contribute to shaping the lives of many students. When I look back at the four decades in the academy I have reason to be proud, for indeed I have taken a discipline from its perception as a simple service discipline in 1976, to an acceptance of it as a discipline that awards degrees in Cameroon, whether Bachelors, Master's, or PhDs.

With anthropology graduate students of CATUC during fieldwork (Foumban – Cameroon, 2012)

IKB: *After having talked about setting up anthropology as a respected discipline in Cameroon in this chapter, in the next, Prof focuses on the creation of the Pan-African Association of Anthropologists – the PAAA.*

Chapter 3

The Pan-African Association of Anthropologists (PAAA) and Collaboration with Others

IKB: *Now let us to talk about your role in the discipline within the broader context of the African continent, especially regarding the Pan-African Association of Anthropologists, the PAAA. Since you were instrumental in creating this association, could you tell me more about it, e.g., why it was created in the first place, what steps were taken to create it, whether it is for all of Africa or just sub-Saharan Africa, and its objectives, among other things?*

PNN: While I was in the Ministry of Scientific Research I was sent on a mission to the University of Leiden in the Netherlands, more precisely to the Institute of Environmental Research, because we were designing a program on the environment at the Institute of Animal Research in Cameroon. So, as Deputy Director of Scientific Research I led the team that went to this school of environmental studies at the University of Leiden. While there, the head of that institute, who was sitting across the table and talking to me about cooperation between the Dutch university and Cameroon, asked me, 'Are you going to the congress of the International Union of Anthropological and Ethnological Sciences taking place in Zagreb, Yugoslavia?'[25] I told him I didn't know about it. And then he said, 'Ok, fine. If you didn't know and you want to go, we are organizing a panel during that meeting on the environment, and you can be one of our participants.' And they asked if I could present a paper on the gas explosion at Lake Nyos[26]. So, I did a paper, and then they handled all the expenses. They flew me to Yugoslavia, lodged me, fed me, and so I had a chance to participate. That was my introduction to the International Congress of Anthropological and Ethnological Sciences (ICAES).

IKB: *Can you remember what year it was?*
PNN: 1988. That was my first time attending it, although I had known that the union was established in about 1932 – 1933, and they had held a series of conferences. Here I was, attending the twelfth conference thanks to somebody in the environmental sciences interested in the anthropological input in understanding what happened in Lake Nyos. So, while I was doing my presentation, I found other Africans from Nigeria, Kenya, Ghana, and South Africa. They had come to the presentation because they had read from the conference program that I

---

[25] Even though Zagreb is the capital of present-day Croatia, the event narrated here took place when Croatia was still a part of Yugoslavia.

[26] On 21 August 1986 carbon dioxide emissions exploded from the bed of Lake Nyos, located in Menchum division (in the North West Region of Cameroon), killing over 1700 people and more than 3000 livestock – see Guern, Shanklin, and Tebor (1990).

was going to talk about the Lake Nyos gas explosion. At the end of my presentation, they came to me and said, 'Well, it is a fascinating subject that you have just presented,' and so we left there, and we walked out: Professor Dike was there from the University of Nigeria, Nsukka; Professor Ocholla Ayayo from the University of Nairobi; Professors George Hagan and Albert Awedoba from the University of Ghana; and then the famous South African anthropologist who became British, Adam Cooper.

We went off to a café to get some coffee. As we sat around the table and we began to chat, others in the café kept glancing at us, probably wondering who these Africans were. There were 1,200 anthropologists attending that conference, and our discussions revealed that there were just about fifteen Africans who had made it there. We eventually, at the end of the conference, caught up with for example Robert Thornton from the University of Witwatersrand, and a couple of others. Anyway, we sat around the table and wondered where the Africans were at the conference. You had all these bigger groups like the Indians, the Americans were dominating the entire conference etc., and then the Europeans. So, we began to ask, 'Where are the Africans?' Another big question involved Africa as a field of anthropological research. The point is that Africa, beginning from the emergence of anthropology as a discipline, was one of the most important fields in which experimental or ethnographic research had been taking place. Africa for a very long time had been used as a laboratory for anthropological experimentation. Western anthropologists usually came to Africa to study our different cultures.

So, we asked ourselves and one another, 'How can we as one of the major field stations for anthropological research be absent in such a major thing as this conference? Here is a big conference with 1,200 anthropologists from all over the world, but who and where are the Africans?' And when we were talking Africans, we did not just mean those African people who had the black skin colour, the dark tone, whom you could easily identify with Africa, but also people like Cooper and Thornton who were white South Africans, whom we also considered as Africans. And as we sat together drinking coffee, we all decided that we needed to fish out Africans, maybe there were African anthropologists who were in different universities all over Africa, but we did not know them.

As I explained before, my participation at the conference had been coincidental, because if I had never been working in the ministry, I would never have been sent on this assignment to the University of Leiden to talk to people about the environment, and they would consequently not have been able to identify me and bring me to the conference. So, there was the possibility that there were many other Africans who would not have had such an opportunity like I had had. We then decided that we would split up into smaller groups, visit all the panels at the conference, and try to identify any Africans. Of course, one key identification would be their skin tone! If they were black, we would presume they are

Africans. In this way we finally identified about fifteen of us.

IKB: *(At this point Prof goes to a shelf in his office and pulls out an old folder. He brings this to where we have been sitting, places it on his desk, and ruffles through its pages to find information on the PAAA. Prof later showed me this folder and I saw that it was the original agreement and draft of the association. It contained the names of all the founding members and their universities, their statement creating the Association, and some rules and regulations.)*

PNN: Mmhmm… Then we concluded that we would do something about the visibility of African anthropologists in the world and decided to produce a statement. Let me read the statement to you, the statement coined by African anthropologists attending the twelfth ICAES:

'We take this opportunity to congratulate the organizers of this congress who made it possible for so many anthropologists to assemble from all over the world to interact, and exchange ideas and viewpoints. We want to express our deepest gratitude to the organizations and foundations that made it possible for us to participate at this conference. It is unfortunate that so few of us Africans could come, and that African ethnology and anthropology did not feature as prominently as it should have. This is clear evidence that African anthropologists are confronted with serious problems. Those of us who are here feel that we need to come together and identify our problems more clearly. For this purpose, we have decided to explore the possibilities of forming an Association of African Anthropologists. As an initial step a steering committee has been constituted. We seek the support of this world gathering in this endeavour.'

The first signature on the sheet was mine; the second was that of Dr Alabi A. Fagbemi, a medical doctor living in France; the third signature was that of George Hagan from the Institute of African Studies, University of Ghana; the fourth was Albert Awedoba's also from the Institute of African Studies, University of Ghana; the fifth was Dr Ocholla Ayayo's from the University of Nairobi, Kenya; then the sixth person to sign was Kofi Agorsah – department of History, University of West Indies in Mona; and the seventh person was Dr Adama Diop from the department of History, University of Dakar Senegal; the eighth person was Mamadou Diawara, Frobenius Institut, Frankfurt; the ninth was Dr Zaongo from the Centre of ethnolinguistic research in Ouagadougou; and then Dr Azuka Dike from the department of sociology and anthropology, University of Nigeria, Nsukka; then we had Dr and Mrs Shehu, department of Geography, University of Sokoto, Nigeria; and then Dr Akuffo, department of African development studies, University of Zambia in Lusaka.

So, we all signed that statement, which to me was the turning point. From among us a steering committee was created. I was selected as the chairman of that steering committee and empowered to convoke a conference at the University of Yaounde. We also decided that at that forthcoming meeting we would create an association with a strong executive. The meeting would take place in Yaounde in1989, and the theme would be *'The Situation of Anthropology in Africa'*. This would permit us not just to do an inventory of departments that existed in Africa but also and inventory of anthropologists in these departments, the different programs offered, and even consider the issue of publications.

So, we presented the statement at the closing ceremony of the conference, and as we walked off the stage, a lady immediately followed us. She introduced herself as Dr Silverman, and said, 'If you are serious, we will provide the funding for your conference'. She was the president of the Wenner-Gren Foundation. In this way, funding, which would have been our biggest challenge, was instantly made available. At this point, we decided that before the meeting in Yaounde, the steering committee would draft a constitution, which would be presented and hopefully approved by the general assembly. We also decided to invite regional representatives from East Africa, West Africa, and all the countries in Central Africa.

IKB: *Why did you choose to focus only on these three regions of Africa? What about Northern and Southern Africa?*

PNN: It wasn't that we chose to focus on these areas. What happened was that upon returning to Cameroon from the ICAES and acting as the appointed chairman of the steering committee we had set up in Zagreb, I made efforts to reach out to universities throughout Africa. I virtually wrote to all vice chancellors of African universities asking them to identify and send anthropologists teaching in their universities to attend the first conference of African anthropologists to be held in Yaounde. We received positive responses mostly from universities in East, West and Central Africa. That is why the constitutive general assembly of the Pan African Anthropological association (PAAA) was made up of scholars from these regions. The other regions such as Southern Africa and North Africa would affiliate themselves later.

Now you did ask me a question about what the main purpose and objectives of the association were. The objectives laid out at the time were to:

- Promote development, research, and teaching of anthropological and ethnological sciences in Africa.
- Facilitate the exchange of students and faculties among departments of anthropology
- Encourage the exchange of research results through documentation and therefore the establishment of a journal. I will talk about the journal later
- Promote a better understanding of African civilization and studies
- Study cultures and societies of African peoples
- Protect the values of African people
- Conserve those values, and therefore, foster the promotion and conservation of African material culture

I would like to elaborate that the steering committee to prepare for the conference in Yaounde was composed of five people: me as the Chairman of the committee, Hagan from Ghana, Ocholla Ayayo from Kenya, Adama Diop from Senegal, and then Dike from Nigeria. They instructed me to contact the vice chancellors of all African universities. Our plan was to simply tell them, 'Don't worry, we have enough money to cover the cost. Just identify the persons to attend the conference we are planning to hold in Yaounde.' Again, the availability of funding was very helpful. So, upon my return to Yaounde, I discussed the idea with the director of Scientific Research, Mr Jean Nyagachou, and the Minister who at that time was Abdulaye Babalaye. Both were very understanding and decided to support the organization of the conference.

At that time there were very few universities in Africa. Cameroon had only one university, Nigeria and South Africa had a lot fewer than they do now. So, as I said before, I identified these universities, wrote to the Vice chancellors, and received responses from 35 of them, to whom we sent invitations for their anthropologists to attend the conference.

The first conference of African anthropologists therefore took place from 03 – 06 September 1989 in Yaounde, Cameroon. The event was sponsored by the Wenner-Gren Foundation for Anthropological Research and was convened by me, the interim chair of the ad hoc group created in Zagreb, Yugoslavia. The purpose of the conference was to assess the current state of the teaching and practice of anthropology in Africa by Africans. A total of seventeen papers were presented, including assessments regarding the discipline and practice of anthropology in Benin, Botswana, Cameroon, Central African Republic, Chad, Ethiopia, Ghana, Ivory Coast, Kenya, Madagascar, Mozambique, Niger, Nigeria, Senegal, Tanzania, Togo, and Zambia. Many of the participants revealed in their papers that anthropology was little known or appreciated in their respective countries, and that they were struggling to make the discipline more central to their universities' curricula. They also emphasized the potential use of anthropological research in development and called on decision makers to recognize that potential.

Prof Nkwi addressing participants at the first conference of the Pan-African Anthropological Association (PAAA) (Yaounde – Cameroon, 1989)

The conference ended with the creation of the Pan-African Association of Anthropologists, that is the PAAA, the adoption of a constitution, and my election as the association's first president. An executive committee was also elected. The members included Dr A.B.C. Ocholla Ayayo from Kenya as first vice president, Dr Adama Diop as second vice president from Senegal, then George Hagan from Ghana as the secretary general, Dr Sery Dedi from Ivory Coast as assistant secretary general, Dr Ayodele Ogundipe from Nigeria became the treasurer, Dr Makonnen Bishaw from Ethiopia became the conference officer, Dr Titi Nwel from Cameroon and Dr Randrianmandinby Bov-Joana from Madagascar were in charge of publications, and finally Dr Ana Maria Laforte from Mozambique and Dr Azuka Dike from Nigeria were elected as at-large members of the executive committee.

The association decided to start publishing a newsletter every three months, beginning in January 1990. We also decided to start a monograph series.

Another issue of importance was membership, especially regarding students. We pondered whether students should be a part of the organization or not, and also what criteria would be adopted, i.e. would membership apply only to African students whether they were trained in African universities or abroad, or would it apply to students trained only in African universities? It was finally decided that membership in the association would be open to all anthropologists who were citizens of the Organization of African Unity states. That was why it was called Pan-African. However, this did not exclude the fact that there could be regional associations of anthropology like that existing in southern Africa. This latter is a corporate member of the PAAA.

In some of our conferences held in different parts of Africa, we have had people attend from North Africa like Algeria, Morocco, and Egypt. Also, at one time Gaddafi was interested in the organization, but we didn't pursue that. It is a pity we didn't because it could have been a great opportunity to widen the scope and membership as well as resources of the organization.

So, membership is for all Africans in Africa. Africanists in other parts of the world would be encouraged to support the PAAA by joining as associate members for an annual fee of 15.00. This fee would include a subscription to the newsletter.

IKB: *And this was 1500 FCFA[27]?*
PNN: No, $15.00, not 1500 FCFA.

IKB: *Ok, I wonder why the PAAA did not pursue Gaddafi's interest in the organization especially as he was very instrumental and influential in the African Union.*

PNN: Gaddafi, the president of Libya was indeed a visionary and a convinced African of the Casablanca bloc vision of Africa. In the 1960s six Heads of State met in Casablanca under the leadership of the King of Morocco to lay down the foundation for the United Nations of Africa. The six nations that dreamed of uniting Africa in this way were Morocco, Egypt, Ghana, Liberia, Mali, and Algeria. Their vision was to build a united Africa

---

[27] The currency used in some countries in Central Africa, like Cameroon, Central African Republic, Gabon, and Congo.

under one command, one currency, and one political governance. By the time the group met in Monrovia to establish a viable economic entity, more African colonial territories had become independent and they were hostile to the idea. It seems that France had encouraged its newly independent nations to fight against a strong united Africa because this could effectively exclude the interference of colonial powers. Mali, which had opted with the Casablanca philosophy would witness the destruction of its infrastructure by the French before they finally pulled out. The establishment of the Organization of African Unity (OAU) in Lagos in 1963 was a loose body of nations who preferred to remain under the colonial yoke than to have true independence.

African leaders who had nurtured the Casablanca dream have been systematically eliminated: Lumumba, Sankara, Gagbo, and more recently Gaddafi whose dream was to unite Africa. Anyway, it was within this intimidating context that Gaddafi sought to work with Pan-African organizations, and so the PAAA was at one time approached by Libya to join in its effort to revive the Casablanca philosophy. But we weren't very keen on the idea. As a relatively new organization, we needed to sink our roots deep in the soil before seeking potential partners.

It is interesting to note that members of the PAAA right from the start have been active especially regarding the sociopolitical atmosphere of their countries. For example, the year the first PAAA conference held in Yaounde, one of our members became the Deputy Foreign Minister of Madagascar.

Another, Professor Makonnen was jailed by his country for being a radical anthropologist, and we even had to write a protest letter. Also, Dr Hagan became the Commissioner Minister in charge of culture in Ghana and became a presidential candidate in the Ghanaian elections.

IKB: *Can you tell me more about Professor Makonnen's arrest, which, I think, points to the fact that apart from it not being a well-understood and accepted discipline, anthropology was further seen as a threat to the political power of most governments in many emerging African states?*

PNN: Professor Makonnen was a professor at the University of Addis Ababa in Ethiopia who apparently was on the wrong side of the revolutionary government of the new Head of State, Mengistu Hiale Mariam. It was because of his contrary political leanings that he was arrested. Working with the International Union of Anthropological and Ethnological Sciences, the PAAA endorsed a protest letter to the Ethiopian government asking for his release. He was finally released some years later.

IKB: *Ok, and now back to the PAAA*

PNN: Yes. After the first conference, which took place in Cameroon in 1989, the second took place either in 1991 or 1992 – I can't remember exactly – in Nairobi, Kenya. The third conference, which was to take place in Nigeria, didn't hold because of logistical as well as financial problems. Ever since then, the association has been holding its conferences. The last conference, which was the eighteenth conference, took place in Port Harcourt in Nigeria in 2018. Since the conference is usually biennial, the next will be holding this year 2020.

IKB: *In all this time would you say that the PAAA has been successful especially in terms of the objectives you talked about?*

PNN: I must say that the association's presence and its wide membership have had a tremendous impact on the introduction and teaching of anthropology in African universities. There were universities that didn't have anthropology departments, and some universities didn't even entertain the idea of anthropology especially universities in many francophone countries. In fact, delegates in these French-speaking countries like Gabon, Chad, Togo, Benin, and Senegal who used to attend the conference understood much more what anthropology entailed from an Anglo-Saxon perspective. I believe this helped greatly in setting up anthropology departments in their universities. For example, I was invited to Benin to chair a PhD thesis in anthropology by departments that were once known as sociology departments, but now they are combined sociology and anthropology departments, or at the very least sociology departments with a section dedicated to anthropology. In addition, we had a conference in Benin. We also had another in Dakar, and in Libreville. Just the fact that we are moving from one region of Africa to another, and because the more we hold these regional conferences the more we attract local scholars to do papers, is why we persist. We are still alive. You know the Association of African Political Sciences collapsed even though it was once the richest. So, I am happy and hopeful because we have been able to survive.

IKB: *And if you had to pinpoint one thing and say that has been the biggest challenge to you as an association, what would that be?*

PNN: It is making anthropology acknowledged by our own colleagues in the sciences, that anthropology is a discipline in its own right that can help Africa codify its values and norms etc.

Oh! One of the visible achievements of the PAAA has been the establishment of a journal called *The African Anthropologist*. We decided to do this at the second Yaounde conference. Our plan was to produce a volume every year, and a volume was considered to have four numbers.

IKB: *When did this happen, that is the second Yaounde conference and establishment of the journal?*

PNN: I think 1994.

IKB: *And is it produced as often as planned, that is, since 1994 has it been consistent or have there been years where you have not produced a volume?*

PNN: At first it had some teething problems. All through the 1990s it was run from the secretariat in Yaounde, I mean the secretariat of the PAAA. The secretariat is still there in CRADAT. We decided to ensure a better future for the journal by signing a protocol agreement with the Council for the Development of Social Research in Africa (CODESRIA), which meant the editors would do the editing, put the journal together, send it to them, and they would publish. So, they became the publishers. And we continued to do that until 2012.

But then we ran into some problems, problems not generated by the editorial board, but by the incapacity of the publication department of CODESRIA to roll off, because after the 2012 volume, we prepared two more volumes for 2013 – 2014 on sex and sexuality, one in French and the other in English, to cover the two years. Then when we held the conference of the PAAA here at CATUC in 2014 we again prepared another volume to cover 2015. Similarly, in 2016 after the conference in Nsukka in Nigeria we prepared another to cover that year. We sent all these volumes to the publications department, but they haven't been published because of the publishing organization. Something went wrong and they changed the key people in the publications division. However, a member of the new team, Dr. Divine Fuh (a Cameroonian anthropologist) tried to help us especially with the 2016 edition, to make up for the ill-luck we had been having.[28]

Presently, I am determined to resolve those problems and keep this journal, which I call the voice of African anthropology, alive. We need to maintain

---

[28] At the moment, however, Dr. Divine Fuh is lecturer of Social Anthropology at the University of Cape Town, South Africa.

it, and so I am proposing to set up a new editorial board. I am going to resign as editor-in-chief and we will get a new person to be on the editorial board and to keep the journal running, because it is the most visible sign of the PAAA. There are two things that I always say make us feel we are still alive: one is that we organize our conference every two years, and the other is that we keep the journal running. That I think is my greatest source of pride.

IKB: *You also mentioned that apart from the journal you were thinking of doing a monograph series. Did that ever happen?*

PNN: No, we didn't finally do that. Rather we decided at one point in the history of the journal to do special issues like the ones on sex and sexuality I mentioned before. I am hoping we will be able to run another on African marriage traditions. So, instead of running a monograph series, it has been more feasible to run special issues of the journal with invited editors depending on the area of focus among the four subfields of anthropology.

IKB: *Ok, and now what future do you foresee for the PAAA?*

PNN: I think the mechanisms put into the constitution ensure that the organization will keep going, as at the end of every conference there is a flag bearer, or the torch bearer who picks it up and takes it to his country or to his region. For example, when my university hosted the conference in 2014, at the end of the conference Nigeria took the baton and said, 'We will organize it. We will bring African anthropologists to Nigeria.' The host university provides the next president of the association, so it's like an incentive. So, at every conference there will always be a country, a department, or a university that wants to invite us because, once they invite the PAAA it means they take the leadership, and a major element of that leadership is a successful conference.

A short while ago I attended an anthropology conference in Southern Africa where I presented the keynote address. During this conference I had the chance to liaise and to talk with lots of our colleagues, colleagues I knew in the past. And the Southern African group said they would be glad to host the PAAA in the nearest future. It might be in Malawi; it might be Zambia. What is clear is that it will be somewhere in southern Africa. So, in this way, and through the journal, the organization can keep going.

Now, one of the things which I think I am proud of having fostered in my service as PAAA president was my effort to establish a training program for master's and PhD thesis students to provide them with skills and knowledge to compete in international journals and for financial resources to do their research. I came up with this program.

IKB: (*Prof shows me a picture of himself and some of the early master's and PhD students, and as we talk he points to people on the photo.*)

PNN: You see this? All the people in this picture have their PhDs: one, two, three, four, five, six, seven, eight... this training was held in Douala. The guy there (*pointing*), Professor Russell Bernard, is famous for research methods. Russ was one of the trainers.

Prof Nkwi with Prof. Bernard at the American Anthropological Association (AAA) meeting (Washington DC – USA, 2017)

I first met Russ in Zagreb in 1988, and since then we have never parted ways. He was president of the commission called Documentation, which was part of the International Union of Anthropological and Ethnological Sciences. In 1988 the computer was still a mystery, and computers were just getting into anthropology. So, he came to Zagreb and set up some small computers for our use. You could sit on it and type, for example, the Bum people, the Nkambe people, polygyny, or whatever, and something would pop up on the small screen. I was fascinated by it, so I sat on this thing and I started playing with it – I was like a little child playing with a toy. And he walked up to where I was, stood silently for a while, and then said, 'Hey, I have been watching you for some time now. You are probably very much interested in getting this.' I said yes. Then he asked me, 'Where are you from?' I said, 'I am from Cameroon.' And then I asked him, 'Where are you from?' He said, 'University of Florida.' I said, 'That's not possible.' And he said, 'Why is it not possible?' I said, 'I have been to Florida several times as part of government delegations and I have never met you.' He said, 'Well now you'll meet me.'

From there we came up with our first project, which was a language project, and within a couple of months he had got enough money to fly to Cameroon with two computers, and I got a number of teachers together to teach them how to use the computer to write their local languages. Why we had chosen local teachers was because Russ had written ethnographies in local Latin American languages and he wanted to do the same thing in Cameroon. After the project, I said to him, 'Russ, I want to push this to a higher level. I don't want to work just with local teachers. I also wish to train young Africans with master's and PhDs up to the level where they can source for and secure funds, etc.' Then we decided to write a proposal showcasing the need for this kind of training.

Our point was that many people, young Africans especially in anthropology just like me who had come back in 1976, got their PhD, came back to their country, were given jobs, but nobody was there to help them handle the transition into academics. We proposed that a project should be carried out where we could bring a minimum of ten Africans with PhD or master's degrees to teach them how to become professionals in anthropology; not only to compete for journal space and publish, but also compete for resources and make themselves more visible and more marketable. So, we wrote the project and got $200,000 to run a program for three years, which would train a cohort of anthropologists over a three-year period.

The program was to be run in three main phases. In the first phase we would concentrate on teaching grant and proposal writing. At the end of this training, participants' proposals would be sent out for competition. If the proposal was successful, then the participant would carry out the research project for which the proposal had been written. Upon completion it would be time for the second phase: data analysis. Data analysis was no more the usual, traditional ethnographic colouring and trying to identify patterns yourself. Now, you were taught how to use the computer to do the sorting out, the focus was on using new technology to enhance our discipline. Finally, the third workshop was called the writing clinic, and its focus was on skills of converting the analysed data to a paper or ethnographic report. Here participants had to write a paper and bring it to the clinic, and we would spend the whole week improving on that paper and showing them how a good paper ought to be written, and how it offered you a chance to compete for journal space.

So, for three years we trained 36 anthropologists. It became so attractive that people who were not anthropologists started applying to take part. We did it in Cameroon and Russ would come all the way from Florida. Also, Wenner-Gren Foundation were willing to support us. My other friends who were keen on doing a lot of things in Africa also came in, especially Professor Ngakutou who was at UNESCO at the time. They were very helpful, and they joined us to train during some of these workshops. UNESCO also supported some of the technical workshops that we organized in different parts of Africa and beyond. At one time we organized a workshop in Porto Alegre in South America, and UNESCO aided us to achieve this. Why I cite UNESCO so much is because UNESCO became very interested in the role that anthropology often played within its programs. And this is the book (*shows me a book*) which is the result of that kind of cooperation. A couple of us were put together to produce this book: *The Cultures of Population, Population Dynamics and Sustainable Development*. It contains an article on Cameroon.

Apart from working a lot with UNESCO, UNFPA were also keen after the 1994 Cairo conference. They were interested in seeing how anthropology could help them understand the cultural barriers to introducing an effective population policy. There was a great woman, Marie-Angelique, who became the director of the African Division of UNFPA. With her and others we began to show that a better understanding of Africans' culture was significantly important, and a few colleagues and I designed a program regarding how to demonstrate how cultural insights were critically important in population mainstreaming. So, you see how my life and my activities were shaped by a whole group of persons and institutions.

Prof Nkwi with President Obasanjo, Nigerian Head of State, at the Network of African Scientific Organizations (NASO) meeting (Nairobi – Kenya, 1986)

IKB: *Moving from the PAAA and collaboration beyond Cameroon, the next chapter looks at the role of anthropology in the context of contemporary issues. Prof focuses on sociopolitical issues and starts by showing how traditional political set-ups can inform modern state-building.*

Chapter 4

Anthropology, Tradition, and Contemporary Sociopolitical Realities

IKB: *At this point we are going to talk more about your assertion that anthropology is still relevant in today's world by focusing on the modern nation-state. What are your thoughts regarding traditional political systems and traditional African political thinking in today's world?*

PNN: One of the thoughts which began to occur to me while I was still studying, and even when I started working and used to joke with my students about being a Marxist, is that the West, in its imposition of political structures and political institutions on Africa, failed to understand that African countries were not functioning without structures prior to the Westerners' arrival. These African communities were governed. They had a system. Nobody has taken time to look at that closely. Even though the African Institute based in London attempted to produce monographs of various kinds, like those about African political systems, African systems of studies, kinship, etc., that massive information has never been used to inform the emerging African political system.

Sometimes I joke that basically in the African DNA you don't become a chief for a limited period of time. You are given your chieftaincy for life, and you relax. While you relax others govern, right? Others govern. And if you want to abuse your authority, they take you out. Nobody has examined that. Now I may come in, elect a president, give him five years. By then he is very comfortable. Then within five years I start telling him, 'You have to go.' Now he begins to look for crooked ways to stay in power and that is what most of our African leaders have done. Why can we not say we have a president until he dies, fine, but there will be a whole series of institutions and structures that ensure that he doesn't abuse that power?

IKB: *Like the kwifoyn[29] in traditional societies*
PNN: Exactly. The fon is for life. Even with the members of the *kwifoyn* we keep renewing the membership and reassigning functions. This is just part of what I thought regarding African political thought, that this is an area we have not fully explored. And the pragmatism of it is that all solutions are now going to the theory of functionalism – every cultural factor has a function to play, right? If it has a function to play, we can improve on that function. We cannot just eliminate it. We bring in elections, and the elections are not what we Africans think they should be, because elections mean one man one vote, but our traditional leaders are not elected, they emerge.

---

[29] Also 'kwifor', 'kwifon', or 'kwi'nfon'. A popular male regulatory society in many traditional kingdoms of the northwestern Grassfields of Cameroon – see Funteh and Gormo (2020); Nkwi (1985).

IKB: *Can you say more about the role of kwifoyn and other such organizations in traditional politics, for example in Kom, and how you think this kind of government set-up can inform modern state formation?*

PNN: *Kwifoyn* is a regulatory society among the Kom people. It was indeed a traditional governance structure or form of government, which took different names like the *nwerong* and the *ngumba*, among the Tikar groups of the northwestern Grassfields. As a governing instrument, it had several lodges specialized in different functions (royal household, economy, diplomacy, ritual and religious duties, judicial and administrative functions). The Indirect Rule policy was inspired by these types of political and social institutions that the British colonial administration found in operation in the different colonies. Instead of replacing traditional instruments of governance with British modes of governance, the colonial administration simply used the existing traditional institutions, which they referred to as Native Authorities, to govern the colonies.

Although Native Authorities played a vital function during the colonial period, unfortunately they are either largely ignored or misused by local politicians nowadays whose disdain for traditional authority usually seeks to take away any remnant of power these Native Authorities once had. *Kwifoyn's* role has been relegated to rites and rituals, with very little input in the domain of modern governance. This is sad, really, as traditional political set-ups can be a profound resource for state-building.

Prof Nkwi's (centre) initiation as a full member of the male regulatory society, the *kwifoyn*, after 16 years of being tutored in the *Kom Academy of Culture and History*, where he was taught by many including Bobe Ngong Nange (first from left), Bobe Anchang (second from right), and Bobe Nchintoh (first from right). Nchindo Anguo (second from the left) served as Prof's assistant during the three days of initiation (Kom palace – Cameroon, 1992)

IKB: *You also talked about African Pragmatic Socialism and linked it to the theory of functionalism. Can you elaborate upon the relationship between the two?*

PNN: Functionalism, as a theory, whether structural or social, asserts that each human society is composed of parts or units, and each of these units plays a vital function in the maintenance and harmonious functioning of the whole entity. Radcliffe-Brown's structural functionalism deconstructs human society into its composite parts that reflect the composite parts of a biological organism. Also, when Malinowski builds his functionalist theory on the vital needs of each society, he asserts that the necessity of these vital needs (feeding, housing, order, etc.) leads to the creation or the invention of appropriate ways to satisfy them. Drawing from these two, African Pragmatic Socialism builds on the inherent nature of the composite parts of all African societies, and is based virtually on the *ubuntu* philosophy – I exist because you are.[30] Any society has basic needs and the fulfilment or the achievement of our collective future requires the contributions of all. For me African Pragmatic Socialism is a process of engaging or harnessing the potentials of local communities towards the achievement of a better quality of life for all. Meaningful change of a given society must be based on the internal values and vision, and not imposed by external forces. Enculturation occurs when members of a given society assess the benefits of an incoming cultural value and ascertain its higher degree of performance, otherwise that element is rejected.

African Pragmatic Socialism recognizes the need of living in a community and is conscious of the roles to be played as required by the whole community. The individual is not an independent isolate but a vital

---

[30] 'ubuntu ngumuntu ngabantu' – 'a person is a person through other persons': the pervasive African philosophy built on a foundation of communalism, which explains that each human exists in relation to and with others, and identity is constructed not in terms of the individual but in terms of the community. Thus, we as human beings are responsible for one another – see Kotzé et al (2012).

element of a functional community; (s)he is nothing without the community, whether this is understood to be the family, lineage, clan, chiefdom, or modern state. The concept of sharing binds the members of a community. The functional nature of that community then depends on the part played by different composite units.

Consequently, the role of an anthropologist who studies a given society is not to fold his/her hands and do nothing, but to be concerned with the quality of life of the people (s)he is studying or has studied. Informants in those communities were the ones who taught us about their culture. We used the information to become what we are, i.e. PhD holders with comfortable jobs that provide us with a decent life. Africanist anthropologists, upon leaving the field may spend years publishing about their research communities with little or no thought of giving back to those communities. This is against African Pragmatic Socialism, which encourages the moral responsibility of researchers to improve upon the quality of life of the people who provided them with the research knowledge. African anthropologists who have studied their own communities cannot be indifferent to the plight of their people. Giving back to the community becomes an even greater responsibility for them.

Over the years I have attempted to give back to my community because what I am today is because they were and still are. I carried out field work from 1973 to 1974. I defended by thesis in 1976 and by October of that year I was hired as the first lecturer in anthropology at the lone University of Yaounde. Four years later I became Program Officer in the General Delegation of

Scientific and Technical Research, and within a year of my first appointment I rose to the rank of Deputy Director of Scientific Research, a post I held for eight years. Conscious of my role as an indigenous anthropologist I began to work closely with local elite groups to find solutions to basic human problems. My commitment and involvement in local development associations like KBDA and NADA became a necessity. From 1996 to 2006 I was engaged with local elite associations in the improvement of local road infrastructure, schools, and health.

As part of my effort to give back to the community, I obtained authorization from the government to create a technical secondary school in 1989. My vision was to provide an education that would train local technicians in building and construction, electricity, computer science, woodwork, and secretarial skills. The school which I had mentioned before, Georgian City Academy, did not only provide affordable tuition, it also gave possibilities to parents to provide technical education to their children in the community. In the 30 years of its existence, the school has trained hundreds of young men and women in these technical areas. In addition, in 2002, in an effort to stimulate the local economy and increase financial accessibility of women, I pioneered an effort to create a microfinance enterprise (MC2 Njinikom), which has over 4000 members and a capital of over 2.000.000.000 FCFA today. Making a difference in our respective communities is a moral obligation based on what that community did to shape us into what we are.

IKB: *Having already applied this way of thinking to you work, what do you think is a concrete way through which these ideas of African pragmatics can inform politics in the wider African society?*

PNN: Recent history of modern African politics has shown us how Western democracy has been tropicalized. Once in office, political leaders will do everything to stay in power either by rigging elections or physically eliminating their political opponents, and above all manipulating national constitutions, constitutions based on Western models. Heads of state and leaders of political parties have ossified their position and would prefer to stay in power for life. The inborn or innate concept in traditional African political systems, as I aforementioned, is that the chief or fon is on the throne for life, and so can only be removed by death. In the past in the northwestern Grassfields of Cameroon especially among the Tikars, for instance, the male regulatory society, be it the *kwifoyn, nwerong,* or *ngumba* took measures to control a chief's potential abuse of power. If they were not successful, and the ruler misused or abused his power, then these regulatory societies made him disappear, because it was only upon his death that another could be crowned in his place. Thus, ruling was for life.

Contrarily, Western democracy limits the term of office and requires a chief to cease to be chief and become an ordinary citizen. You can then clearly see how this will not work well. Nowadays, politicians often use strategic ethnicity (tribalism) to mobilize their kinsmen during Western-styled elections. Public property and positions have been tribalized, and state resources are often distributed depending on ethnic consideration. Imagine an African country where in a cabinet of more than 60 ministers, more than 30 are members of the same ethnic stock, and a majority of the officers recruited into the army or military is from that ethnic stock. Africans have adopted democratic institutions from European contemporaries but refuse to live up to the democratic rules that inform these institutions.

IKB: *Indeed, I can very well see how in this new hybrid, the idea of giving up power in Western democracy might be at loggerheads with the African traditional political notion of ruling for life. Also, I wonder how you handle being an anthropologist in your current position as a member of the Constitutional Council. Can you share your thoughts about how relevant anthropology is in your work within the Council?*

PNN: My appointment to the Constitutional Council was, as I said before, one of the greatest surprises of my life. When I retired in 2006, I returned to my region, the North West, and settled in Bamenda; I was fed up with living and working in Yaounde. But that appointment on 07 February 2018 brought me right back to Yaounde. My immediate reaction was thinking about how to use the anthropological knowledge I had acquired over the years to contribute to the work of the Council. When I discovered that the preamble of the constitution was built around the linguistic and cultural diversity of the nation, as well as *'the protection of minorities'*, and the preservation of the 'rights of indigenous populations in accordance with the law', it became clear to me that I had a role to play.

As a non-jurist my participation in the work of the Council is often well appreciated by my colleagues. It is important to note that of the 69 articles of the constitution, six of them specify the duties and functions of its members, namely assuring the constitutionality of laws, treaties, and international agreements. Since becoming a member, it has been a learning process.

IKB: *During this learning process, what have you found out concerning the role that anthropology can play in the modern state of Cameroon?*

PNN: The preamble of the constitution asserts its pride in 'our linguistic and cultural diversity, an enriching feature of our national identity'. Anthropology as a discipline studies precisely linguistic and cultural diversity of world populations. Ethnographic studies of the over 300 ethnic groups in Cameroon is the object of anthropology, and the contribution of anthropology to understanding this diversity should be this: the construction of a modern state cannot ignore these diversities if it wants its development strategies to have any meaning. The fact that the modern state of Cameroon approved the teaching of anthropology at the university level has shown its interest in a better understanding of its peoples and cultures.

IKB: *Ok, and having worked as an anthropologist and been prominent in the political landscape of Cameroon for a while now, what are your thoughts about the role of anthropology in addressing the ongoing sociopolitical issue – the Anglophone Crisis[31] – in Cameroon?*

PNN: I think the Anglophone crisis was the outcome of a failure to accept diversity and build it into the national fabric. Cameroon, besides having over 300 linguistic and cultural groups, inherited both the British and French cultural proclivities during colonialism. However, it seems that Cameroonian politicians of the French expression have over the last 50 years attempted to annihilate Anglo-Saxon values and to destroy any trace of bicultural nature (French and British) within Cameroon.

It is interesting to note that the two colonial systems, i.e. the French Direct Rule as opposed to the British Indirect Rule, were imposed on Cameroon after the Germans pulled out. The Indirect Rule policy, which was based on anthropological knowledge, was effective in British Southern Cameroon, where the British ruled through the Native Authorities. Conversely, the *'mission civilisatrice'*, i.e. the civilizing mission, which informed

---

[31] A sociopolitical crisis centering around what anglophones perceive as their marginalization by the predominantly francophone government and military of Cameroon – See Anchimbe (2018), Doho (2020), and Fonkeng (2019) for a more in-depth analysis of this and other crises currently plaguing Cameroon.

French colonial policy, imposed direct Jacobian rule of the French while ignoring local values of the colonies. When the French finally opted for Indirect Rule at the Brazzaville Conference of 1945, it was too late and African populations under the French were already used to being told what to do.

When the Federal Constitution of Cameroon was drafted in 1961, the intention was to maintain the values brought by each party, i.e. the francophones of French Cameroon and the anglophones of British Cameroons, to the union. Apparently, the francophone politicians had a secret agenda, which was to dismantle the structures and institutions inherited from British Southern Cameroons. The Federal Republic of Cameroon created in 1961 would become the United Republic of Cameroon in 1972, ignoring the Anglo-Saxon values. Similarly, the emergence of the Republic of Cameroon in 1984 would complete a slow and deliberate policy of total assimilation or annihilation of any vestiges of former British Southern Cameroons.

Over these 50 years deliberate attempts were made to eliminate any traces of Anglo-Saxon educational and juridical systems. The policy of harmonization of educational programs and the overbearing presence of francophone judges in anglophone courts would betray the hidden policy of the Biya regime to annihilate anything anglophone. The teachers' strike and that of lawyers in 2016 was a manifestation of the rejection of any further harmonization. The arrest of anglophone leaders and their eventual incarceration would begin a process of regaining the pre-1972 Southern Cameroons autonomy. During a conference in Paris in 2019, President Paul Biya acknowledged that the Anglophone Crisis was indeed due to Anglophones refusing to become assimilated. Attempts at decentralization have proven to be futile efforts which will not solve the crisis. Instead they have aggravated the situation. From an anthropological lens, I believe that a return to the 1961 Federal Republic may offer a solution to the crisis even though many still believe secession is the optimal outcome.

IKB: *In the final chapter, Prof shares his thoughts about the possible future of anthropology both in Cameroon and Africa.*

Chapter 5

Applied Anthropology – the Future of Anthropology in Africa

IKB: *In talking about sociopolitical issues, setting up the discipline of anthropology in Cameroon, and working as part of the PAAA, you stressed the importance of applying anthropology to several fields.*

PNN: Yes. I think many of the anthropologists both in Cameroon and Africa are currently working in areas where applied anthropology is required, mostly because they are struggling to survive. In the applied areas they can act as consultants and work on projects. Also, quite a few of them have been pulled out of academic institutions to head institutions which are not fundamentally anthropological. Take one of my former students who is head of the International Union for the Conservation of Nature, i.e. the IUCN, in Cameroon. He did a PhD under my supervision but now he is the country representative of IUCN. Others are working in a variety of areas where they are making use of applied anthropology.

This brings me to the famous debate, or indeed outright disagreement sometimes with some of our colleagues in well-endowed universities, who have enough money to spend on theory construction and theory creation. In summary, the three main stances within the discipline of anthropology are the Ivory Tower, Schizoid, and Advocacy views. Today these three viewpoints can be seen in many areas around the world. The Ivory Tower perspective says that there is no anthropology outside the university because fundamentally anthropology is simply an academic discipline. So, whatever occurs beyond this setting is not anthropology. Proponents of this view explain that anthropology is originally an academic study of different cultures and people around the framework of the university, where anthropologists collect data, analyse it, speculate on it, draw conclusions, and generate theories from these conclusions. Therefore, anthropology should be situated within the university.

Then we come to the Schizoid. The Schizoid anthropologists say, 'We are anthropologists. We cannot remain in the Ivory Tower. We need to go out there and play a role in informing those who are trying to transform human social life and make people's lives better. We do this by carrying out ethnographic research among communities, and then providing the findings regarding their social and cultural situation to those who wish to make the communities' lives better, thus helping these latter to understand the communities better. So, our role is to provide the knowledge, but we are not responsible for its application. If they make a mistake in the application, they will not blame us.'

Then the Advocates explain, 'Look here, you hire me as an anthropologist. I have the training. I have the skills to provide the kind of information you need. I come into your organization and you employ me full time. I collect data, I analyse it, I provide findings, and I know how to apply them. I don't tell you what to do and step aside. So, I provide the knowledge and am an integral part of its application.' These anthropologists work in organizations, they do research, and they attempt to make big changes in those organizations and the communities they work in and with.

There are those who criticize anthropologists in Africa. They say that we don't practice anthropology because not much theory is being generated by us. This critique has sometimes driven some of us to cook up theories whose foundations are so sandy that they don't stand the test of academic and intellectual discourse. Given the reality we face in Africa, from the very beginning, the PAAA stood very firm and constantly promoted the last two – the Schizoid and the Advocacy. The reasoning behind this is that while we remain in the Ivory Tower, because that is where we craft or generate theories and ideas, we should not forget that the people we are speculating upon need to live a better life, and we need to strive to help them achieve this. So, throughout these past 30 years or so, I believe the Schizoid and the Advocacy group have become the dominant trend among African anthropologists. These are the applied anthropologists.

IKB: *How efficient and effective would you say that this way of practicing anthropology has been in shaping the Cameroonian society?*

PNN: I think applied anthropology has been a visible marker of the discipline and has greatly contributed to changing people's perception of the discipline. The increasing number of students signing up to study anthropology in Cameroonian universities is a clear indication that we have successfully demonstrated the role anthropology can play in nation-building. Therefore, people like you, people like me, we are into anthropology, we can make a living, we are participating in national debates as anthropologists, and people get to appreciate that. My interventions on national issues as an intellectual, but more as an anthropologist, have always been appreciated by people, and I think this is where we can be proud that our discipline can make a difference.

Anthropology in Cameroon is not the same as it was 40 years ago when I began teaching. A lot of changes have occurred. Today, the people I have trained over these 40 years are the ones – young people like you - who are stepping up, who are understanding the role of anthropology in national reconstruction, and who are the sign that things have changed. You could say that anthropology, and not just Cameroonian but also African anthropologists, have contributed immensely to changing the mindset of policy makers, development-oriented people, and people-centred actions/projects. The number of anthropologists working within the NGO world is indeed an acknowledgment that we have a role to play in society.

IKB: *Indeed. So, if you had the chance to pinpoint one thing and say, 'this is the legacy I am leaving behind in relation to anthropology' what would that be? In other words, what do you* *hope to be remembered for in relation to anthropology in Cameroon and Africa?*

PNN: At the level of the continent I think I am proud to have been the founding president of the PAAA. I am proud that at least that flame is still flickering and that my legacy is in the young people who are joining the discipline, and who I do pray and hope, will keep that flame burning. It usually gladdens me immensely when I travel around the continent, go to universities all over Africa, and find that their anthropology departments are being recognized and are flourishing. There is no country that I go to now and say I am an anthropologist, and they don't say, 'Well, we also have anthropologists here.'

A few years ago, I went to the University of Malawi, Zomba. The Vice Chancellor came on stage to open our conference and said, 'Next year we want to examine the possibility of creating an anthropology department in this institution. People like Professor Nkwi visiting us really inspires us to start our own department. Secondly, I do not understand why the Catholic university 40 kilometres away has a department of anthropology, and we don't.' As I listened, I was very proud... very proud and happy. Also, the Catholic University of Zambia has a department of anthropology. They started about ten years ago. I was so proud of the people who left there and came to the conference, two young people teaching there. That is the kind of legacy I like to look back on and think that the future will be brighter, especially if some of the people we train get into areas of policymaking that can make a difference at the continental level.

In the same vein, my legacy for Cameroon is the number of students that I have trained. I can vouch that almost everybody who can be counted as an anthropologist in Cameroon would say they thank Prof for being there, because if you go to the Universities of Buea, Douala, Yaounde, and now CATUC, you will find my students running their anthropology departments. I am happy to see that we have a new generation taking over, and after this one there is a whole new crop of PhD students that I produced who will take over and keep the flag flying. I can comfortably exit knowing that anthropology will be in good hands.

Equally, one of my greatest legacies is the creation or establishment of the department of anthropology at CATUC, because I couldn't believe that having nurtured the creation of the department in other institutions around the country, at the end, I wouldn't create one here. At CATUC, in addition to the greater liberty and control I had as part of the think tank which set up the university, I was surrounded by people who at the very least shared my mindset, and so it was easier to start up a department of anthropology at the institution. One of the things I am going to leave is my entire library to the CATUC, because it will be useful in this setting, and my collection of books will be well looked after by my grandkids in the anthropological family. I am very, very proud that although it is a very small department with fewer numbers at the undergraduate and greater numbers at the graduate level, qualitatively they are really good. I know that there are some people who call me the father of Cameroonian anthropology, and that isn't farfetched.

The future of anthropology in Africa is bright. Many universities are opening departments of anthropology and many of our students are turning their attention to the study of their own cultures. When I look back at the few students in 1976 and the hundreds that fill our lecture halls today, I have reason to believe that the discipline will continue to make its mark.

Prof Nkwi at a Youth Football tournament of Georgian City Academy (Njinikom – Cameroon)

cell pattern forms? Is it maintained throughout
their lives? [...]

[...] through [...] the pores [...] [...] build
[...] and one [...] edge, [...] the conditions which
[...] implement and [...] out the cells [...] it are
there [...] in the [...] cells [...] that, even without
[...] the [...] it may [...] maintain [...]? And if a
[...] of [...] other [...] a [...] like it. Cannot
[...] to [...] the place [...] a [...] minute [...]?
[...] [...]

Concluding Remarks

Ivoline Kefen Budji

Looking at the conversations I had with Professor Nkwi, narrated within these pages, it is evident that he was not simply a product of his time, but a pacesetter, who ushered in a new era especially regarding anthropology in Cameroon. In line with Dureau's (2014) critique of the statement (which has been ambiguously used sometimes as an excuse and at other times as a call for academic generosity) that several earlier anthropologists were people or reflections of their times, I believe anthropologists are called to, if they can, transcend those times to become visionaries and trailblazers, who use their work to predict, inform, and usher in positive change. Past events inform current realities and future actions. As the conversation in this work has shown, Prof Nkwi has set the pace and opened a path for anthropology not just in Cameroon, but most parts of Africa. Prof's elucidations presented here illustrate changing trends in Anthropology in Cameroon and beyond, through colonialism to postcolonialism, and from modernity to postmodernity. The wealth of information contained in his responses is as historical and contemporary as it is anthropological. In the narrative of Prof's life is found a summary of the anthropology of Cameroon, indeed qualifying him as the 'father of Cameroonian anthropology'.

During this historic period in the world when we are facing a global pandemic, i.e., the coronavirus pandemic, and its related health, sociopolitical, and economic challenges (cf. Nkwayep et al 2020; Washington 2020), and the anglophone regions of Cameroon are further experiencing the Anglophone Crisis, which traces its roots to the country's unique and complicated colonial history (cf. Anchimbe 2018; Fonkeng 2019), the importance of anthropology cannot be overrated or understated. As illustrated in the present work, which while chronicling a complicated past is also a call to greater awareness of the salient importance of anthropology, African anthropologists can use knowledge of the past and the discipline's in-depth, iterative, interactive, reflexive, dynamic, and holistic characteristics (cf. Devisch 2011; DeWalt and DeWalt 2011; Jegede 2015; Olukoshi and Nyamnjoh 2011) to address these and other contemporary issues and challenges, forge a brighter path for the future, and provide key insights into the human condition by variously demonstrating what it means to be human.

I therefore think it is apt to end with this quote:

The future of anthropology in the decades ahead will depend on how anthropology meets the challenges of the 21st century. One of the major challenges is meeting the needs and demands of a fast-changing world. The rehabilitation of its image is well on the way to full recovery, but the integration of anthropological insights into the development process of African nations must become a permanent and not just an ephemeral feature (Nkwi and Messina 2015: 27 – 28).

Afterword

Paul Nchoji Nkwi

When I retired in 2006 from teaching at the University of Yaounde I, I least expected that one day my teaching and involvement in anthropology would be the subject of discussion. But thanks to Ivoline whom I met in 2011 at the new Catholic University in Bamenda, this unforeseen event has become reality. As one of my brightest graduate students she was inquisitive and interested in auditing my career as an anthropologist. At first, I was reluctant, but she was tenacious, pointing out that it was important for posterity. This book is therefore the result of many hours of conversations and reflections about the intertwinement of my life's journey and career as a postcolonial anthropologist.

References

Anchimbe, E., (2018). 'The roots of the Anglophone Problem: language and politics in Cameroon.' *Current History* 117 (799), pp. 169 – 174.

Apter, A., (1999). 'Africa, empire, and anthropology: a philological exploration of anthropology's Heart of Darkness.' *Annual Review of Anthropology* 28, pp. 577 – 598.

Ardener, S., (1996). 'Foreword', in Fowler, I., and Zeitlyn, E. (eds.) *African crossroads: intersections between history and anthropology in Cameroon*, Vol. 2. Berghahn Books, pp. ix – xvi.

Asad, T. (1993). *Genealogies of religion: discipline and reasons of power in Christianity and Islam*. Baltimore: Johns Hopkins University Press.

Barnard, A., (2001). 'Africa and the anthropologist.' *Africa (pre-2011)* 71 (1), pp. 162 – 170.

Basu, P., (2016). 'N.W. Thomas and colonial anthropology in British West Africa: reappraising a cautionary tale.' *Journal of the Royal Anthropological Institute* 22 (1), pp. 84 – 107.

Devisch, R., (2011). 'What is an anthropologist?' in Devisch, R., and Nyamnjoh, F., (eds.) *The postcolonial turn: [re-imagining anthropology and Africa]*. Bamenda: Leiden, Netherlands: Langaa Research and Publishing CIG; African Studies Centre, pp. 91 – 115.

DeWalt, K. M., and DeWalt, B. R., (2011). *Participant observation: a guide for fieldworkers*. 2nd edn. New York: Altamira Press.

Doho, G., (2020). 'From literary concept to self-proclaimed state: three generations of Anglophone-Cameroonians at war.' *Journal of the African Literature Association*, pp.1 – 20.

Dureau, C., (2014). 'Acknowledging ancestors: the vexations of representations,' in Hviding, E., and Berg, C., (eds.) *The ethnographic experiment: A.M. Hocart and W.H.R. Rivers in Island Melanesia, 1908.* New York: Berghahn, pp. 44 – 70.

Fonkeng, P., (2019). 'Insecurity, forced migration, and Internally Displaced Persons along the Cameroon-Nigeria Border, 2003-2018.' *AfriHeritage working paper.*

Fowler, I., (2011). 'Kingdoms of the Cameroon Grassfields.' *Reviews in Anthropology* 40 (4), pp. 292 – 311.

Funteh, M. B., and Gormo, J. (2020). 'Women, conflict, and peace in the Grassfields of Cameroon.' *Africana Studia* 13, pp. 91 – 113.

Gardner, L. A., (2010). 'Decentralization and corruption in historical perspective: evidence from tax collection in British colonial Africa.' *Economic History of Developing Regions*, 25 (2), pp. 213 – 236.

Guern, F. L., Shanklin, E., and Tebor, S., (1992). 'Witness accounts of the catastrophic event of August 1986 at Lake Nyos (Cameroon).' *Journal of Volcanology and Geothermal Research* 51 (1), pp. 171 – 184.

Irvine, J. T., and Gal, S., (2000). 'Language ideology and linguistic differentiation,' in Kroskrity, P. V., (ed.) *Regimes of language: Ideologies, polities, and identities*. Santa Fe: School of American Research Press, pp. 35 – 84.

Jegede, A. S., (2015). 'From gateway to gatekeeper: anthropology: yesterday, today and tomorrow,' in Nkwi, P. N., (ed.) *The anthropology of Africa: challenges for the 21st Century*. Mankon, Bamenda: Langaa RPCIG, pp. 3 – 12.

Jindra, M., (2005). 'Christianity and the proliferation of ancestors: changes in hierarchy and mortuary ritual in the Cameroon Grassfields.' *Africa* 75 (3), pp. 356 – 77.

Kallaway, P., (2012). 'Science and policy: anthropology and education in British colonial Africa during the inter-war years.' *Paedagogica Historica: Gender and Education in History* 48 (3), pp. 411 – 430.

Kotzé, E., Els, L., and Rajuili-Masilo, N., (2012). '"Women ... mourn and Men carry on": African women storying mourning practices: a South African example.' *Death Studies* 36 (8), pp. 742 – 766.

Mafeje, A., (1976). 'The Problem of anthropology in historical perspective: an inquiry into the growth of the Social Sciences." *Canadian Journal of African Studies/La Revue Canadienne Des études Africaines* 10 (2), pp. 307 – 333.

Mbembe, A., (2015). 'Decolonizing knowledge and the question of the archive.' *Public Lecture, Wits Institute for Social and Economic Research*, University of the Witwatersrand in Johannesburg.

McGee, R. J., and Warms, R. L., (2017). *Anthropological theory: an introductory history*. 6th edn. Lanham: Rowman & Littlefield.

Ndi, A., (2016). *The golden age of Southern Cameroons: vital lessons for Cameroon.* Denver: Spears Media Press.

Ndong, G. K., Nde, V., and Nguo, V. L., (2015). 'Focus on the World Bank safeguard policies and the Chad-Cameroon oil and pipeline projects.' in Nkwi, P. N., (ed.) *The anthropology of Africa: challenges for the 21st Century.* Mankon, Bamenda: Langaa RPCIG, pp. 101 – 110

Nkwayep, C. H., Bowong, S., Tewa, J.J., and Kurths, J., (2020). 'Short-term forecasts of the COVID-19 pandemic: a study case of Cameroon." *Chaos, Solitons and Fractals* 140. https://doi.org/10.1016/j.chaos.2020.110106

Nkwi, P. N., (1979). 'Cameroon Grassfield chiefs and modern politics.' *Paideuma* 25, pp. 99 – 115

Nkwi, P. N., (1985). 'The Kom palace: its foundation, growth and significance." *Paideuma* 31, pp. 105–110.

Nkwi, P. N., (2015a). 'Introduction: the anthropology of Africa: challenges for the 21st Century,' in Nkwi, P. N., (ed.) *The anthropology of Africa: challenges for the 21st Century.* Mankon, Bamenda: Langaa RPCIG, pp. Ix-Xiv. Mankon, Bamenda: Langaa RPCIG, pp. ix – xiv

Nkwi, P. N., (2015b). 'Welcome speech,' in Nkwi, P. N., (ed.) *The anthropology of Africa: challenges for the 21st Century.* Mankon, Bamenda: Langaa RPCIG, pp. 621 – 624.

Nkwi, P. N., and Messina, C., (2015). 'Anthropology at the University of Yaounde: a historical overview: 1962-1999,' in Nkwi, P. N., (ed.) *The*

anthropology of Africa: challenges for the 21st Century.
Mankon, Bamenda: Langaa RPCIG, pp. 13 – 34.

Nkwi, W. G., (2015). *African modernities and mobilities: an historical ethnography of Kom, Cameroon, c. 1800-2008.* Baltimore, Maryland: Project Muse.

Nyamnjoh, F.B., (2012). 'Blinded by sight: divining the future of anthropology in Africa; die erforschung des elefanten: zur zukunft der ethnologie in Afrika." *Africa Spectrum* 47 (2-3), pp. 63 – 92.

Olukoshi, A., and Nyamnjoh, F.B., (2011). 'The postcolonial turn: an introduction,' in Devisch, R., and Nyamnjoh, F.B., (eds.) *The Postcolonial turn: re-imagining anthropology and Africa.* Bamenda: Leiden, Netherlands: Langaa Research and Publishing CIG; African Studies Centre, pp. 1 – 27.

Ortner, S. B., (1984). 'Theory in anthropology since the sixties.' *Comparative Studies in Society and History* 26 (1), pp. 126 – 166.

Ortner, S. B., (2016). 'Dark anthropology and its others: theory since the eighties.' *HAU: Journal of Ethnographic Theory* 6 (1), pp. 47 – 73.

Stambach, A., (2010). 'Education, religion, and anthropology in Africa." *Annual Review of Anthropology* 39 (1), pp. 361 – 379.

Vigh, H. E., and Sausdal, D. B., (2012). 'From essence back to existence: anthropology beyond the ontological turn.' *Anthropological Theory* 14(1), pp. 49 – 73.

Washington, H. A., (2020). 'How environmental racism is fuelling the coronavirus pandemic.'

Nature 581 (7808), 241.
https://doi.org/10.1038/d41586-020-01453-y

PAUL NCHOJI NKWI

CV and Publications

Name: **PAUL NCHOJI NKWI**
Nationality: Cameroonian

ADDRESS: Catholic University of Cameroon (CATUC)
P.O. Box.782 Bamenda
Cameroon
Tel: mobile (237) 737 8494
Tel. Mobile (237) / 96167396
Tel mobile (237) 5025 4000
Email: nkwi70@yahoo.com

EDUCATION

1964-1967	BA Philosophy. Bigard Memorial Seminary. Enugu, Nigeria.
1967-1971	BA Theology/. Pontifical Urban University, Rome, Italy.
1971-1974	B.A. (Hons) Anthropology. University of Fribourg. Switzerland
1974-1976	Doctorate (Anthropology). University of Fribourg, Switzerland
1981-1982	HABILITATION (Post-doc Anthropology). University of Fribourg., Switzerland

TEACHING POSITIONS HELD

1974-1976	Teaching Assistant, University of Fribourg, Switzerland
1976-1977	Assistant Lecturer, University of Yaounde, Cameroon
1977-1983	Lecturer, University of Yaounde, Cameroon
1983-1993	Associate Professor, University of Yaounde, Cameroon.

1991-2010	Professor of Anthropology, Yaounde University, Cameroon
Since 2010	Professor Emeritus, University of Yaounde I, Cameroon
2010-2018	Professor of Cultural Anthropology, Catholic University of Cameroon

SENIOR ADMINISTRATIVE AND PROFESSIONAL POSITIONS HELD

1980-1981	Programme Officer, Ministry of Scientific Research, Cameroon.
1981-1984	Deputy Director, Programmes, Ministry of Scientific Research, Cameroon
1984-1987	Deputy Director, Scientific Research, Ministry of Higher Education and Scientific Research (MESRES), Cameroon
1987-1988	Acting Director, Department for Scientific and Technical Research, Ministry of Higher Education and Scientific Research, Cameroon.
1988-1990	Senior Adviser, Ministry of Higher Education and Scientific Research, (MESRES) Cameroon.
1990-1993	Senior Adviser, University of Yaounde, Cameroon.
2000-2005	Executive Director, African Population Advisory Council, Nairobi, Kenya
2010-2016	Deputy Vice Chancellor for Academic Affairs, Catholic University of Cameroon (CATUC), Bamenda, Cameroon
2018	Member of the Constitutional Council of Cameroon

POSITIONS HELD IN FOREIGN UNIVERSITIES AND INSTITUTIONS

1981-1982	Visiting Professor, University of Fribourg.
1982	Senior Fulbright Scholar, University of Columbia, South Carolina.
1983	Fellow, Alexander von Humbolt, University of Frankfurt.
1986	Senior Fellow, African Studies Centre, University of Leiden.
1991	Visiting Professor, Harvard University, Harvard Medical School.
1993	Temporal Adviser, External Review Team, World Health Organization, Diarrhoea and Acute Respiratory Infection Programmes.
1995	Visiting Professor, Rhodes University, Grahamstown, South Africa
1997	Visiting Professor, Center for African Studies, Univ. Of Florida, Gainesville
1998	Visiting Professor, University of Bergen, Norway
2000-2006	Executive Director, African Population Advisory Council, Nairobi, Kenya

MEMBER OF PROFESSIONAL ASSOCIATIONS

Fellow, Royal Anthropological Association of Great Britain.

Fellow, African Academy of Sciences.

Founding Fellow, Cameroon Academy of Sciences.

Member, American Anthropological Association.

Member, Society of Applied Anthropology (USA).

Founding President, Pan African Association of Anthropologists 1989-1998.

Vice President, Network of African Scientific Organization

Member, Future Action Committee for Africa.

Member, Network of African Medical Anthropology.
Member, Network of African Population Anthropologists
Executive Member, Social Science and Medicine Africa
Network (SOMA-Net)
Executive Member, International Union of
Anthropological and Ethnological Sciences;
Executive Member, International Social Sciences Council,
UNESCO, Paris
Vice President, African Academy of Sciences,
Member, Union of African Population Studies
President, Pan African Anthropological Association (2005)
Member, World Council of Anthropological Associations
(WCCA since 2007)
Executive Member, International Union of
Anthropological and Ethnological Sciences
Vice President, Conglomerate of Microfinance Institutions
(AMC2) in Cameroon
Executive Member of the African Academy of Sciences
President, Council of Elders, Mutual Finance for
Development (MUFID)

CONSULTANCIES

1978	USAID. Socio-Economic Study of ZAPI de l'Est District, Cameroon.
1979	USAID. Village Characteristics of Northern Province, Cameroon.
1984	World Bank. Social Indicators of Cameroon Forest Project.
1988	African Academy of Sciences. Report on Scientific and Technical Research in Cameroon.
1989	WHO. Health System Research Project in Cameroon.
1992	UNDP/FAO. Socio-anthropological Aspects of Environmental Management in Cameroon.
1992	World Bank. African Population Advisory Committee (APAC) Action Programme for the Improvement of the

	Quality of Life in Four Cameroon villages.
1993	Family Health International (FHI). Measuring Adherence to the Policy and Standards of Contraceptive Use, Cameroon.
1993	World Bank, GEF (Global Environmental Facility). Environment Assessment of Socio-economic Indicators, Cameroon.
1993	The World Bank, GEF. Pre-appraisal Mission, Community Participation and Involvement in the Design and Implementation of GEF Biodiversity Conservation Projects in Cameroon.
1993	The Work Bank. Appraisal Mission, Cameroon Biodiversity Conservation Projects.
1994	United Nations Population Fund(UNFPA): Anthropological perspectives of Population Problems in Sub-Saharan Africa
1995	EXXON: Environmental Assessment of the Chad/Cameroon Pipeline Project: Socio-cultural aspects and impact on the project.
1996	UNFPA: Consultant for Fathers Incorporated, Kingston, Jamaica, UNFPAJamaica Country Office
1996	UNFPA Workshops on the Traditional Practices of Reproductive Health: Good and Harmful Practices among Cameroon Ethnic Groups. UNFPA, Cameroon.
1996	Study of Infertility among the Tribes of the East Province of Cameroon
1996	UNFPA training Workshop on qualitative Methods in Reproductive Health for Malawian Social Scientists, Lilongwe, Malawi
1998	Social Analyst for the Dutch Centre for

	Environmental Impact Assessment of the Chad-Cameroon Pipeline
1999	Centre for Environmental Assessment, Utrecht, The Netherlands. EIA Chad Cameroon Pipeline
1999	Global Environmental Facility (GEF), Cameroon, Reorientation of the Campo-Ma'an Project
2000	Department for International Development (DFID) Review of C ommunity Forests Initiatives
2000	WHO Cholera Emergency Team to Madagascar: My TOR were to look at the cultural factors enhancing the spread of the cholera Epidemic.
2001	USAID/CARPE Evaluation Report, conducted with the Environment and Development Group, Oxford, England
2001	Human Rights Law Group, Washington, Preparation of NGOs of Congo Democratic Republic for their participation for the International Conference on Racism, Durban
2001	National Democratic Institute, Preparation of Opposition Parties for their participation in the Inter-Congolese Dialogue, Kinshasa
2002	Consultant for Culture and Development, Development of the Cultural Policy for the Government of Eritrea, Asmara
2003	Consultant for the design of UNFPA's African Social Research Program. The Socio-Cultural factors that propagate or prevent the spread of HIV! AIDS
2007	Consultant, UNESCO for the Establishment of the Institute for African Culture and International Understanding, Abeokuta, Nigeria
2008	Consultant, UNESCO for the

	Establishment of the Centre for Black
	Culture and International Understanding,
	Osun State, Osogbo, Nigeria
2009	Consultant, UNESCO, New Cultural
	profile for Member-States of UNESCO
2009	Consultant for OCPA, Organisation for
	Cultural Policies in Africa, Mozambique
2007-2009	Consultant for the Bamenda Ecclesiastical
	Provincial Conference of Bishops
	(BAPEC) for the establishment of a
	Catholic University

PUBLICATIONS

Articles

1975a "The clan in the process of change" in *Ethnologische Zeitschrift*, Band II, Zurich, pp. 35-48.

1975b "The return of a Stolen God" in *Abbia* (Yaounde), pp. 121-128.

N/D "The origin of Kom Matrilineal Institutions" in *Symposium Leo Frobenius*, pp. 127-138. Deutsche UNESCO Kommision.

1976 *Christianity in Kom : Its Foundation and Growth*. Afo-a-Kom Publications Yaounde.

1977a "Changing attitudes among a Grassfield People" in *Cahiers du Departement de Sociologie*, Vol. I, No. 1, pp. 40-50.

1977b "Kinship structure among the Kom of the Bamenda Grassfields" in *Cahiers du Departement de Sociologie*, Vol. I, No. 2, pp. 12-27.

N/D *Margui-Wandala Division (Cameroon): An Annotated Bibliography*. USAID, Yaounde.

1979a *ZAPI de l'EST. A socio-economic analysis*. Dept.of Sociology, Uni. of Yaounde.

1979b "Chiefs and Modern Politics" in *PAIDEUMA*, Mitteilungen zur Kulturkunde, Weisbaden, No. 25, pp. 99-115.

1979c "Food Crop and Market Participation in Kom" in *Agricultural Marketing in the North West Province*, USAID,

Washington, pp. 432-440.

1980 "The Lake Nyos Gas Explosion: Different Perceptions of the Phenomenon" in *Discovery and Innovation*, Vol. 2, No. 2, pp. 7-19.

1981 "Traditional Female Militancy in a Modern Context" in J.C. Barbiers (ed) *Femmes d'hier d'aujourd'hui*, CNRS (Centre National de la Recherche Scientifique), Paris.

1982a "Meta Political System" in J.C. Barbiers (ed) *Nature et Forme de pouvoirs dans les societes dites Acephales*. ORSTOM (Office de la Recherche Scientifique et Technique d'Outre Mer), Paris.

1982b "Some Ethnographic Notes on a Cameroon tribe, (The Maka)" *ANTHROPOS*.

1984a "Slavery and Slave Trade in the Western Grassfields" in Chem-Langhee (ed) *Slavery in Cameroon*. *PAIDEUMA*, Frankfort.

1984b "Traditional Female Militancy in a Modern Context" in J.C. Barbiers (ed) *Femmes du Cameroon*. ORSTOM, Karthala, pp. 182-191.

1985a "The Kom Palace: Its Foundation, Growth and Significance". In *PAIDEUMA* 31, pp.105-110.

1985b "The changing Role of Women and their Contribution to the Domestic Economy in Cameroon" in David Parkin (ed) *Transformation of African Marriage*. International African Institute, London.

1988a "Bridging the Gap between Scientists, Industrialists and National Governments: The Case of Cameroon", in T.T. Isoun (ed) *Mobilization of African Scientists Talents for Development.*, Academy Science Publishers, Nairobi, pp. 55-63.

1988b "Integrating Higher Eduation and Scientific Research in Africa with a view of maximising the use of available resources for greater productivity: The Cameroon Experience" in T.R. Odhiambo & T.T. Isoun (eds) *Science for Development in Africa*. ICIPE (International Centre for Insect Physiology and Ecology) Science Press, pp. 83-92.

1989a "Cultural Dynamics and Identity of the Western Grassfields of Cameroon" in Lukas Sosoe (ed) *Identite: Evolution ou Difference*. Editions Universitaries, Fribourg

Suisse, pp. 209-258.

1989b "The Epileptic among the Bamileke of Maham in the Nde Division, West Province of Cameroon" in *Culture, Medicine and Psychiatry*. Harvard, 13, pp. 438-448.

1989c "Traditional Uses: Risks and Potentials for Wise Use" in M. Marchand & H.A. Udo de Haes (eds) *The People's Role in Wetland Managements*. Leiden, Centre for Environmental Studies, pp. 339-344.

1990 "Becoming Foyn Among the Kom of the Cameroon Western Grassfields" in *PAIDEUMA*, 36, pp. 235-245.

1992 "Funding of research in Africa" in *Science in Africa*, edited by American Association for the Advancement of Sciences, pp. 25-42.

1994a "Perceptions and Treatment of Diarrhoeal Diseases in Cameroon" in *Journal of Diarrhoeal Research*. Harvard, Harvard Institute for International Development.

1994c "What does African Anthropology Need to survive in the next decades?" In *Journal of African Anthropology*, Vol.II, Number 1

1996a "The Ethnography of Development: An African anthropologist's vision of the development process" in *The Cultural dimensions of global change: An Anthropological approach* (ed) Lourdes Arizpe, Paris, Unesco Publishing

1996b The Ethnography of infertility among the Cameroon Tribes of the east Province, in Report Submitted to UNFPA, Country Office

1996c "Ethnicity and Party Politics in Cameroon" in *Regional Balance and National Integration in Cameroon*, eds. P. Nkwi & F.B.Nyamnjoh

1997a "Rethinking the Role of the Elite in Rural Development: The case of Cameroon " in *Journal of Contemporary African Studies*(JCAS), Vo.15 Number 1 pp.67-86

1997b "The royal Art of Cameroon" in *Plundering of Africa's Past,* ed. Peter Schmidt

1997c "Football, Politics and Power in Cameron", Entering the Field, eds.Ben T.Amstrong, & R. Giulianotti, Bergs Publishers pp,123-139

1998 "Contributions of Social Sciences to the Tropenbos-Cameroon Programme", in Seminar Proceedings

Research in Tropical Rain Forests : Its challenges for the Future, Tropenbos Foundation, Wageningen, The Netherlands, pp,125 - 137

1998 "The status of Anthropology in Africa" in *Sociological Review*, pp.1-9

1998 "The anthropology of Africa: Some landmarks and critical issues", in *African Anthropology*, Vol. 5 No.2

1999 A Requiem for a Culture: Media Invasion of Africa, in Media and Social Perception, edited by Enrique Rodriguez Larreta, UNESCO –ISSC Publication, pp.356-376

2001 "Society, Culture and Population in Cameroon" in *Cultures of Populations, Population Dynamics and Sustainable Development* by Sabiha H.Syed (ed) UNESCO Publication, pp.25 – 70

2003 "The Impact of cultural practices in the spread of HIV/AID" a paper presented at the 4th UAPS conference in Tunis,

2006 "Anthropology in a Postcolonial Africa: The survival debate" in *World Anthropologies, Disciplinary Transformation within systems of Power*, by Gustavo Lins Ribeiro and Arturo Escobar (eds), Berg Publications, Oxford, New York, pp. 157 -180

2008   "Healing Trajectories of People Living with HIV/AIDS" in Proceedings of Conference on 20th Year of Research into HIV/AIDS , Abidjan, Cote d'Ivoire

2012 *"Culture, Behavior and AIDS in Africa"* in: Aids and the State in Africa, ed. by. Timothy Quinlan, Ogun Oge, and Paul Nchoji Nkwi. KwaZulu Natal, South Africa: University of KwaZulu Natal

2012 *"Applied Anthropology: giving back to communities that made us what we are"* in Practicing Anthropology in Development Processes: New Perspectives for a radical anthropology *by Floriana Ciccodicola and Paolo Palmieri, Rome, Italy*

2018 Anticipating African Cultural Policies by 2030: A Transversal Study, OCPA paper

Books and monographs

1966 *Kom Marriage Customs*. Enugu, Nigeria.

1976 *Traditional Government and Social Change*. University Press, Fribourg.

1982 *Elements of a History of the Western Grassfields*. Publications of the Department of Sociology, University of Yaounde.

1987 *Traditional Diplomacy*. Publications of the Department of Sociology, University of Yaounde.

1989 *German Presence in the Western Grassfields*. A.S.C. Leiden, The Netherlands.

1998 The Pan African Anthropological Association: Striving for Excellence, PAAA Publications, Yaounde, Cameroon

2001 Field Research into Socio-cultural Issues: Methodological Guidelines, Yaounde, ICASSRT Publication, UNFPA/UNESCO Publication

2012 "Practising Anthropology/ In Development Process

Co-authored articles

2012 Culture, behaviour and AIDS in Africa" in African Responses to HIV/AIDS Between Speech and Action, University of KwaZulu-Natal Press. Ed. Segun and Tim Quinlan. Russel Bernard co-author4ed this article.

2014 A short cultural History of the Kom People, Bamenda

Printed in the United States
by Baker & Taylor Publisher Services